connect

HOW TO DOUBLE
YOUR NUMBER OF VOLUNTEERS

nelson searcy

WITH JENNIFER DYKES HENSON

D0188317

BakerBooks

a division of Baker Publishing Group
Grand Rapids, Michigan

© 2012 by Nelson Searcy

Published by Baker Books
a division of Baker Publishing Group
P.O. Box 6287, Grand Rapids, MI 49516-6287
www.bakerbooks.com

Printed in the United States of America

Library of Congress Cataloging-in-Publication Data
Searcy, Nelson.
    Connect : how to double your number of volunteers / Nelson Searcy with Jennifer Dykes Henson.
       p.   cm.
    Includes bibliographical references (p.).
    ISBN 978-0-8010-1467-3 (pbk.)
       1. Lay ministry—Recruiting. 2. Voluntarism—Religious aspects—Christianity. 3. Church work. I. Henson, Jennifer Dykes. II. Title.
BV677.S43 2012
253′.7—dc23   2012017860

14   15   16   17   18   7   6   5   4

In keeping with biblical principles of creation stewardship, Baker Publishing Group advocates the responsible use of our natural resources. As a member of the Green Press Initiative, our company uses recycled paper when possible. The text paper of this book is composed in part of post-consumer waste.

To the dedicated volunteers who serve
at The Journey Church.

I am grateful that you show up each week with such enthusiasm to grow in your faith and to serve our Lord. In my nightmares, I see what it would be like if you didn't!

contents

acknowledgments

From Nelson Searcy

In the introduction of this book, you'll read about my journey with what I call the ministry system. I have had to learn (and relearn) the lessons embedded in these pages more times than I'd like to admit. I am merely a two-talent guy who has had the privilege of being surrounded by ten-talent people! My eternal gratitude goes to Jesus Christ for calling me to salvation and later to ministry—I'm honored to be one of his equippers for his church.

While dozens, if not hundreds, of pastors have influenced my thinking on ministry and volunteerism, two stand above the rest: Steve Stroope and Rick Warren. If you don't know their names or haven't read their books, please go to Amazon.com right now and order everything they have written. Steve and Rick, thank you for your personal and ongoing investment in me.

In addition, I would like to especially thank the following pastors and church leaders for influencing my views and shaping my thoughts on ministry: Steve Sjogren, Wayne Cordeiro, Bill Hybels, Bryant Wright, Jimmie Davidson, Tim Stevens, Tony Morgan, Ray Wickham, Milton A. Hollifield Jr., Erik Rees, Lance Witt, Adam Bishop, and Larry Osborne. If the theology and applications in this book are correct, you can thank the pastors above. If there are mistakes, those are solely mine.

I must also express huge thanks to my colleagues at The Journey Church, both past and present staff members. Since 2001, I have had the privilege of being the dumbest person on an extremely smart team. Kerrick Thomas and Jason Hatley, in particular, have greatly shaped the thoughts in this book. To all of our current staff, I love doing church with you! To those God will call to our staff in the future, I look forward to being on the team with you. We have openings right now—get in touch!

My sincere appreciation goes to the team that makes Church Leader Insights happen every day of every week. You have no idea of the impact you are having on pastors around the world. Thank you, Scott Whitaker, Tommy Duke, David Luster, Brendan Vinson, Kimberly Pankey, Vinny Bove, and Jimmy Britt!

I must also express my thanks to the now eleven hundred–plus pastors who have completed one of my Senior Pastors Coaching Networks. Many of the ideas shared in these pages were first beta-tested on you. Your feedback, insights, and improvements have made this a much stronger system. Thank you for living out the "learn and return" principle.

Jennifer Dykes Henson has been a partner on my last eight books. I am so grateful that she initially stepped up in 2004 as a volunteer at The Journey and offered to use her communication skills "to help out as needed." She is now such a valuable part of the team that to say she "helps out" is an understatement. This book simply would not be in existence without Jennifer. Her passion to communicate my basic material in such a profound way is equal only to her commitment to God and the local church. Thank you, Jennifer! As members at The Journey, Jennifer and her husband Brian serve as models of all that I discuss in this book.

This is my sixth project with the tremendously dedicated folks at Baker. My thanks to Chad Allen, Jack Kuhatschek, Rod Jantzen, Michael Cook, and all the fine folks at Baker Publishing who have made this book infinitely stronger than it was when I submitted the original manuscript.

Finally, I must thank the love of my life, Kelley, and my son, Alexander. Kelley and I first met on a blind date in 1992. Her not seeing me in advance gave me a fighting chance, and I'm still grateful for that opportunity. I say this in every anniversary card I've ever given her since our August 6, 1994, wedding (see, I do remember): Kelley—I love you now more than ever! Alexander, who will turn six years old just prior to the release of this book, has benefited so much from the dozens of volunteers who serve each week in Journey Kidz. Each Sunday afternoon, when he has something new to share after his time in Journey Kidz, Kelley and I are again thankful for the investment those volunteers are making in his young life! Alexander: I love you and you are indeed my main man (and yes, I am done writing for the evening, so now we can wrestle). Thank you both for your commitment to this book and your continual support.

From Jennifer Dykes Henson

Thanks, first and foremost, to God for allowing me to have some small part in calling his people to live more purposefully for him. Thanks to Nelson: the magnitude of the work I am privileged to do alongside you continually humbles me. Thank you for answering the monumental call God has put on your life and for inviting me into that ministry with you. And thanks to my husband, Brian: every day with you is better than the last.

preface

Tuesday, 7:45 a.m. Pastor Tim steps into the diner and immediately notices that something is out of the ordinary. Dirty tables sit untouched. A crowd of people waiting to be seated is forming at the front. Tim scans the restaurant and sees David perched on the edge of their usual booth, surveying the breakfast remains of the people who had been there a few minutes before.

Tim and David, a young pastor with whom Tim has formed something of a mentor relationship, have been meeting for breakfast the second Tuesday of every month for at least three years now—always at the same time, always at the same place. Generally the atmosphere is inviting and the service is smooth, but today the classically well-run diner is different. Tim pushes through the chaos at the front to get to David.

"Hey, man," Tim says. David stands up to greet him. "What's going on?"

"Hey, Tim. I'm really not sure what the deal is . . ."

As if on cue, a waiter who often serves the two steps up and starts clearing the dirty table. "Good morning, guys. Sorry about this. Things are crazy today. We're short two servers and one hostess. I feel like a one-man show running this place."

"No worries, friend," David says to the waiter. Then, to Tim, he jokes quietly, "I know the feeling. Running my church lately feels like running a one-man show. I just hope none of my services turn out like this."

Tim chuckles along with David, but the comment concerns him. Once they settle into the booth and order coffee, he asks, "Do you really feel that way, David? About being a one-man show?"

"Well, I have to admit, sometimes I have this nightmare that I show up at church on a Sunday morning and I'm the only one there—no worship team, no ushers, no greeters, no kids workers . . . just me. I mean, our church isn't huge or anything, but things aren't going to happen like they should without volunteers showing up. And I'll tell you, I could use a lot more of them . . ."

David's not the only one who has that nightmare about being the only person to show up on a Sunday morning. I've had it a few times myself. How about you? One thing we learn early on in our work as church leaders is that the church is a volunteer-run organization. Without people who are willing to serve, we can't do what we've been called to do. In fact, when we try to take care of everything on our own, we mess up God's plan by stunting both our people's growth and our church's redemptive potential.

Dream with me for a minute. What would your church look like if you could double the number of people who volunteer? What if a full 50 percent of your people were connected through serving for at least an hour every week? Imagine the ministries that would finally be fleshed out. Imagine the great experience your attenders would have at each weekend service. Imagine the influence you could begin to exert on your community. Abandon the nightmare and embrace this dream. It can be a reality.

God wants the people he has put in your church to be actively engaged in serving. He has no interest in a one-person show. In fact, connecting your people through service is a critical part of your responsibility to disciple them—a necessary element in helping them become a better reflection of Jesus. In the pages ahead, you'll discover how to build a system that will give you an ongoing abundance of volunteers, consistently attract new people, and make sure you don't burn anyone out. You'll also uncover some surprising, contrarian truths about how to encourage a culture of service in your church. For example, I'll describe:

- Why a pre-serving spiritual gifts assessment can be a bad idea.
- Why it's important to let people serve before they are believers.
- How you can ruin your volunteers by overtraining them.
- Why you have to make eager servers take a break.
- Why you never *need* a volunteer for anything.

When there aren't enough hands to do what needs to be done, things break down. Quiet chaos begins to rumble below the surface. God's vision for your church gets buried beneath the urgency of figuring out how to keep all the parts moving. People languish as consumers rather than contributors, missing God's best for their lives. Ministries aren't able to fulfill the missions they were created for. And you, as the leader, run the risk of falling into a dangerous scarcity mentality.

God has a greater plan for your church. Thankfully, he doesn't operate in lack but in abundance. As you learn how to cooperate with God in leading people into a deeper walk with him by connecting them through biblical servanthood, you will begin to see healthy growth in your members and attenders, in all of your ministries, and in your church as a whole. Are you ready to get started?

introduction

I'm a slow learner. The lessons I'm going to share with you in the pages ahead—and the system they led to—have taken me over twenty years to learn. My thinking about ministry started taking shape back in 1993 when I became the pastor of a thirteen-person church on the northern edge of Charlotte, North Carolina. A few weeks into my role as pastor, one of my congregants let me in on a little secret: the night the church voted me in, they were actually voting to keep the doors open. Their options had been to either take on the kid with no experience or shut down the whole operation for good. They chose me. To this day, I'm not sure they made the right decision.

Over the next several months, by God's grace, the church began to grow. The increase was great for the kingdom— we grew mainly by reaching lost people—but bad for me. Why? I was a one-man show. At first, I thought I had to do everything myself. Then I realized that other people would be helpful, but I was too timid to ask. After a few months of the do-it-myself attitude, I realized I wasn't going to be able to keep my head above water unless something changed. So I proceeded to do what many a young pastor has done: I swallowed my pride and begged for volunteers.

Yes, I stood in front of my little congregation every Sunday morning and begged. I begged people to serve in our nursery. (As you can imagine, this wasn't comforting to our first-time families who had just dropped their kids off in the nursery.) I begged people to come in and serve during the week, to help with administrative and maintenance tasks. I begged people to lend a hand in any and every way possible. I even set up a committee to help me beg. In short, I became a professional beggar because, hey, that's what you have to do to get people to volunteer, right?

Begging actually worked well over the short term. By the time I left the church two years later to pursue graduate work, our attendance had grown from 13 to 130, and we had enough volunteers to squeak by. But as you and I both know, begging isn't a sustainable model for the long run. If you live by the beg, you'll eventually die by the beg.

While I was in graduate school, I didn't pastor a church of my own, but I helped out a great pastor who had just started a new church. The experience marked my first foray into church planting. My time with this pastor taught me more about ministry than I knew there was to learn. He understood that *ministry* simply means *to serve*—and when it came to connecting servers, he didn't have a begging bone in his body. Rather, he knew how to cast vision. Instead of pleading with people to serve, he made them want to serve. Volunteers lined up in spades to be a part of our fast-growing church. My role became something like that of a traffic cop, directing people who were eager to serve into various areas of service. I repented for my old begging ways and said "never again!"

After graduate school I had the privilege of serving on staff at one of the largest churches in America. The senior pastor convinced me to leave a PhD program to work on his staff by saying, "You'll get more out of being a part of what's going on here than out of any PhD program in the world." He was right. I got to see the inner workings of a large, healthy church. I had the unique opportunity to study the fruit of a volunteer system I didn't build. I witnessed bright-eyed men and women arriving early to set up tents, chairs, and children's ministry equipment before sunrise and holding mini pep rallies over breakfast to energize the hundreds of weekly volunteers. I remember thinking, "If I ever get a chance to lead a church, this is how I'll approach ministry."

In 2001 God gave me that chance. My wife, Kelley, and I moved from Southern California to the Upper West Side of Manhattan to start The Journey Church in New York City—the church I lead to this day. As I describe in great detail in my book *Launch: Starting a New Church from Scratch* (Regal, 2006), I started The Journey with no money, no members, and no meeting location. (To learn more about *Launch*, visit www.ChurchLeaderInsights.com/connect.) To grow this new church under the headship of Jesus Christ, I had to internalize, synthesize, and systemize all my ministry experience to date. As I think back through what I have learned about ministry along the way, there are three big lessons I can't get away from.

1. I can't lead a healthy church by myself. This humbling truth is actually a blessing in disguise. Not only am I incapable of leading a healthy church by myself (as are you); God doesn't intend for me to. First of all, I desperately need the Spirit of God and the mission of Christ to be my constant guides. Second, I need the people God has put around me to step into the ministry roles he intends for them.

Logistically speaking (and church health notwithstanding), it is possible to handle everything yourself when you lead a church of a hundred people or less. Of course, that's not God's plan—and you likely won't be able to do it well—but it is possible to keep things afloat. Maybe that's why half of the churches in America have an average attendance of one hundred or less. (For more on why churches get stuck at one hundred, two hundred, and five hundred, see my *Growth Barriers* resources at www.ChurchLeaderInsights.com/connect.) If you try to do it all yourself—at any level—you can count on these three things:

- You will be setting yourself up for major burnout.
- You won't experience the kingdom impact God wants for your church.
- You will be robbing the people in your church of the opportunity to find purpose and passion through serving.

Thanks to all I had learned before 2001, I made an intentional decision from day one at The Journey: I decided to humble myself and admit that I couldn't fulfill God's purposes for his new church by trying to do everything on my own. To this day, that's one of the best decisions I have ever made.

2. If I fail to connect people in significant ministry, I am robbing them of the opportunity to grow. In other words, the people in my church will never become the fully developing disciples I long for them to become if I don't connect them in specific, appropriate ministry positions.

This reality made me uncomfortable. You see, I love being a pastor. I love doing the work of a pastor. I find fulfillment in helping people and—I'll admit it—I enjoy being needed. At the same time, I live to see people grow in Christ. My constant pleading prayer is that our church will be a disciple-making church. I wake up in the morning and go to bed at night thinking about discipleship and the systems that can help grow a healthy disciple. (For more on my systems approach to discipleship, see my free ebook *Healthy Church, Healthy Systems* at www.ChurchLeader Insights.com/connect.)

So, for a long time, I lived with the tension of wanting to do all I could for my own fulfillment, on the one hand, and wanting to connect the people in my church to do what they could for the sake of discipleship, on the other. While I still struggle with this tension on occasion, I ultimately found freedom through studying Ephesians 4—the passage in which Paul clearly describes the role of a pastor:

> Now these are the gifts Christ gave to the church: the apostles, the prophets, the evangelists, and the pastors and teachers. Their responsibility is to equip God's people to do his work and build up the church, the body of Christ. This will continue until we all come to such unity in our faith and knowledge of God's Son that we will be mature in the Lord, measuring up to the full and complete standard of Christ. (Eph. 4:11–13)

Humor me and underline "Their responsibility is to equip God's people to do his work and build up the church, the body of Christ." (It's okay. You can write in the book.)

I won't go into a long exegetical and theological discussion of these verses here, but I do encourage you to spend some time with this passage. Personally, as I prayed and sought God's instruction from Paul's writing, I became focused like a laser on one word: "equip." I realized that my chief role as a pastor is to equip the people of my church for ministry. I don't always get to do; I get to equip someone else to do. When I equip and my people do, we both win. I find fulfillment and confirmation from God regarding my calling, and my people find fulfillment and confirmation from God regarding their place of service. Wow!

One minor thought before we look at the third lesson: over the years I have discovered that I am both a disciple and a pastor. As a pastor I am to equip others to be disciples by calling them to Christ, connecting them in service, and challenging them biblically. And as a disciple myself, I am meant to connect with *some* ministries of the church in a deeply personal way (keyword: "some," not all). I do my part and equip others to do theirs. In other words, I equip people for all of the ministries of the church, but I personally commit to doing only a few things.

3. More people are reached for Christ when more people are connected in places of service. In a way this reality is a natural outgrowth of the previous point—but evangelism must be intentional as well as natural. (For more on intentional evangelism, see my book *Ignite: Sparking Immediate Growth in Your Church* [Baker, 2009], and visit www.ChurchLeader Insights.com/connect.)

When people are connected within your church, finding fulfillment and growing in their Christian faith, they will live out their faith more fully outside the walls of the church—which means they will invite more of their non-Christian friends to your services and events. So, connecting your people in service not only deepens the discipleship ministry in your church; it also expands your evangelism outreach.

I have definitely noticed this correlation at The Journey. The more people we get plugged into volunteering, the more people we reach for Christ. Greater numbers of people serving equals greater numbers of people baptized. Only God could have set it up that way.

As I mentioned, I am a slow learner. The three lessons above have taken me twenty years to learn, but I hope to help you discover the truth of these lessons for yourself over the pages of this book. Even beyond my desire to inspire you and educate you, my goal is to equip you—equip you with a specific nuts-and-bolts system that keeps you from doing it all yourself, doubles your volunteer base, and positions you to reach more people for Christ. To that end, here are a few suggestions for how to get the most out of *Connect*:

- Read with a pen in hand. Allow God's Holy Spirit to speak to you as you read, and capture the thoughts he brings to mind on paper. Even if you are reading this book electronically, I encourage you to take notes.
- Read *Connect* with your entire team. Encourage each person to think specifically about how he can work to

implement the details of the ministry system effectively in his area.

- Take a season to study *Connect* with all of your key volunteers—both laity and staff. I can't overstate the importance of having everyone unified behind a common vision for ministry and volunteerism in your church.
- Share *Connect* with a fellow pastor—learn and return. Learn from the pages ahead and then return your knowledge back to the kingdom by recommending *Connect* to someone else you know who wants a church full of eager volunteers.

I would love for this book to open up a dialogue between you and me. Please connect with me along the way for free stuff, more details, and next steps at www.ChurchLeaderInsights. com/connect.

adopting
a ministry
mindset

1

the significance of service

WHAT MINISTRY LOOKS LIKE

The greatest use of life is to spend it for something that will outlast it.

—William James

The greatest among you must be a servant.

—Jesus (Matthew 23:11)

My wife and I go on a date once a month. Between my hectic schedule and all of Kelley's responsibilities, it can be hard to pin down a night, but twosome time is a priority so we do whatever needs to be done to get a date night on the calendar. Sometimes we keep our dates low-key (think pizza and a movie, maybe even on the couch at home), but sometimes we take things up a notch and go to a new play or a trendy restaurant. Whatever we have planned, I am a stickler about ensuring that the details are fleshed out and that everything is in place.

For one of our recent date nights, I made a reservation at a restaurant in town that was, apparently, the hot new place. A few of our friends had been there and they raved about it. Thanks to all the hype, I had to make reservations three weeks in advance just to get a table. When the night came, Kelley and I got dressed up, dropped our son off at a friend's house, and headed downtown. I was impressed as soon as we pulled up to the restaurant. The building was gorgeous. The ambiance inside was warm and inviting. The aromas swirling around were unbelievable. As the hostess led us past a jazz quartet to our table, I just knew that this would be a great night—a perfect night. That is, until our waiter approached the table.

As soon as Henry (I knew his name thanks only to his name tag) walked up, the mood began to crumble. With no greeting and no eye contact, he pulled out his notepad and grunted, "Do you know what you want?" A little taken aback, I said, "Um, no, we actually just sat down. I think we need . . ." Before I could finish my sentence, Henry shoved his notepad back into his pocket and walked away.

Now, I can dismiss such behavior at a dive or a diner like the place Tim and David frequent, but this place was neither of those things. Not by a long shot. This restaurant was meant to be an experience—the kind of place where you spend time with the menu, ask questions of the waiter, and make sure you choose the perfect dish. It's the kind of place where you linger over your appetizer before the meal comes and linger over your meal before dessert. You get the picture. Saying Henry's attitude did not match the atmosphere is an understatement. He was our server for the evening, but I knew immediately he had zero interest in serving us. He was there out of obligation and the need for a paycheck. His heart wasn't in it.

Our experience with Henry—which only went downhill from there, I'm sorry to say—got me thinking about the whole idea of serving. In Matthew 23:11 Jesus makes a pretty ironic statement: "The greatest among you must be a servant." We're all familiar with that statement—maybe you've even taught a message based on it—but when we drill down, what does "being a servant" really mean? What is the actual connection with "the greatest" among us? Specifically, for our purposes as church leaders, what does Jesus's statement mean in our churches?

The church is unique in that it is largely a volunteer-run organization. People who are willing to serve are crucial to what we do. But a lot of frustration and unanswered questions are inherent in that fact. Questions like: How do we get people to serve? How do we make people *want* to serve, so we don't have a bunch of Henrys showing up out of obligation? How do we best utilize the people who are interested in serving? How do we make sure they want to keep serving? In short, how do we mobilize people for significant ministry?

If you're like me, at some point you have probably looked around at other churches and wondered why they seem to have more volunteers than you do. You've wondered why their people are so dedicated to serving the church, when you feel like you are doing everything on your own, afraid to ask for help. Maybe you've always thought that eager volunteers were directly linked to the charisma of the pastor, or the result of some clever terminology he uses when asking people to serve. Maybe you've wondered if they bribe their people with free ice cream. You can admit it; we've all been there.

The truth is that the leaders at those churches with a plethora of eager volunteers aren't doing anything rare or difficult. They aren't doing anything that you can't do just as well. An abundance of volunteers, or a lack thereof, comes down to one simple thing—namely, the quality of the ministry system operating in the church. As one of the eight systems at work in every healthy church, the ministry system is the system that asks the question just mentioned: *How do we mobilize people for significant ministry?* In case you aren't familiar with my operational theory when it comes to church organization, let me give you a quick rundown of the thinking behind the eight systems of a church.

Defining the System

Those of you who are parents know the awe that comes with holding your newborn baby in your arms. Even though babies are born every day, each one is a miracle. Think back to the last time you looked at ten tiny fingers and toes, or watched a little chest move up and down, drawing breath. By cliché, that baby is a "bundle of joy," but she is also a bundle of something else. She is a bundle of perfectly formed, intricate systems that are already working together to keep her alive.

Thanks to her tiny circulatory system, her heart is pumping blood through her veins. Thanks to her respiratory system, her lungs are taking in air. Her digestive system is breaking down her mother's milk from the very first drop and her muscular system is letting her wrap her little hand around her father's finger. Even in a brand-new baby, each of these systems and others are fully developed, fully functioning, and ready to grow with her as she starts her journey toward adulthood.

God is into systems. He organized the universe with systems. He established the measurement of time through a system. And, from the beginning, he formed our bodies as a cohesive unit of systems. Adam and Eve—unblemished specimens of God's craftsmanship—were compilations of the systems that caused them to function. They were perfect adult examples of that newborn baby. Without systems humming under the surface, they would not have been able to walk or even breathe. They wouldn't have been able to experience the pleasures of the garden. Eve wouldn't have been able to pluck the apple from the tree and Adam wouldn't have been able to take the bite that set God's redemptive plan into motion. Without their systems, they would have remained as unmolded lumps of clay, unable to fulfill the purposes of God. From the beginning, God has put systems to work, providing the mechanics and the platform through which he shows his greatness.

One more thing about Adam and Eve. What is it that we know about them for sure? What was the blueprint God used in creating them? Himself. Genesis affirms that God created man in his own image. Don't miss this: God created beings who function through systems and said that they had been created in his own image. God is into systems.

Paul understood God's affinity for systems. That's why, in trying to help us wrap our minds around how the church should function, he compared the body of Christ to the human body. He aligned the design of the church with the functioning of our own different parts. In Romans, Paul writes, "Just as each of us has one body with many members, and these members do not all have the same function, so in Christ we, though many, form one body, and each member belongs to all the others" (Rom. 12:4–5 NIV). Sounds remarkably like how God designed our physical bodies with systems, right? Go back and read the verse again, substituting the word "systems" every time you see the word "members." It makes perfect sense. All the parts of the body—both the church body and the physical body—work together, allowing us to fulfill God's purposes and plans on this earth. And both of those respective bodies function best through well-developed systems.

A system is any ongoing process that Saves You Stress, Time, Energy, and Money, and continues to produce results. Good systems function under the surface to keep things running smoothly so that you can concentrate on more important priorities. Thankfully, you don't have to think about the fact that your neurological system is allowing you to read and process this information. That system is doing its job, or you wouldn't be able to understand the words in front of you. But if you began to see a decline in your cognitive ability—if all of a sudden you could not remember or analyze information in the way you always have—you would have to deal with the stress of knowing something was wrong and put a lot of money, time, and energy into figuring out where the breakdown was occurring. We may not be aware of a good system when it is running well, but there is no mistaking when something isn't working like it should.

The same is true in the church. We know that the church is a body, so it follows that the church also has systems working beneath the surface. I contend that the church is made up of eight systems: the worship planning system, the evangelism system, the assimilation system, the small groups system, the ministry system, the stewardship system, the leadership system, and the strategic system. Each of these systems is present in your church, whether it is healthy and active or not. And each system is giving you the results it has been designed to give you. If you want to change your results in any area, change the corresponding system in cooperation with the Holy Spirit. (To learn more about all eight of these systems, download the free "Healthy Systems, Healthy Church" report at www.ChurchLeaderInsights.com/connect.)

Recently I've become a runner. When I first started running, my cardiovascular system was not very strong. It was there, but it wasn't used to working efficiently. I could only run a few minutes at a time before I was spent. But over the course of a few months, with directed training, I strengthened my cardiovascular system (not to mention my respiratory system and muscular system), and now I can run long distances without stopping. While I'm proud of my progress, I have a friend who has been running for years and can still run marathons around me. His cardiovascular system is more highly developed than mine. So, while we all have a cardiovascular system—you, me, my friend the marathoner—they are in different stages of health based on what we do to exercise and maximize them. See where this is going?

In the same way, as church leaders, we all have a ministry system at work beneath the surface of our church. In some churches, this system is more highly developed than in others. The churches with well-developed ministry systems are the churches that always have plenty of volunteers who are willing and eager to find a place of service and dedicate themselves to it. These are the churches that are able to attract many more volunteers than they even have room for—which is a great problem to have—and who understand that wise recruitment of volunteers is actually a form of discipleship.

The ministry system is an ongoing system that motivates people to serve for the first time and mobilizes them for a lifetime of serving. Unlike some of the other more independent church systems, the ministry system is a far-reaching system. It affects every other system. Just as a cardiac failure would be devastating to the other systems in your body, a weak ministry system inhibits every area of your church. Why? Because the ministry system is where you discover the servants whose time and efforts will go a long way toward making your church effective. It's where you find the people who will head up your small groups system; it's where you find the people who will make your assimilation system run well; it's even where you identify people who may become future staff members at your church. Your church can't operate without volunteers, so the strength of the system by which you mobilize people for service is crucial. To that end, there are four clear steps to creating an effective ministry system:

1. Clarify your theology of ministry.
2. Create first-serve opportunities.

3. Cultivate a ministry ladder.
4. Celebrate and reproduce servants.

While the remainder of these pages will focus on the details of implementing these steps and moving people through processes, I don't want you to miss the ultimate truth behind this discussion: at its core, the ministry system is about helping people become servants. The word "ministry" simply means *to serve*. Woven into every principle and strategy in this book are Jesus's words, "The greatest among you must be a servant." The way we cooperate with the Holy Spirit to help our people become servants—which ultimately helps them become fully developing followers of Jesus—is to provide them with the knowledge, tools, and opportunities they need to give themselves to something greater than themselves.

> *The ministry system is an ongoing system that motivates people to serve for the first time and mobilizes them for a lifetime of serving.*

In a Word

Back in 2002, when we started The Journey, we understood next to nothing about the importance of systems within the church. We launched on Easter Sunday with 110 people in a comedy club on New York City's Upper West Side. The next Sunday I learned an inherent truth of church leadership: not everyone who shows up on Easter Sunday comes back to church the next week. Over the next three months, through my dynamic leadership and charismatic preaching, I decreased the church down to thirty-five people. That's when I began to realize certain things we needed to do in order to cooperate with God in the work to which he calls us.

That fall, things began to turn around. One of the early signs we'd rounded a corner happened just before Thanksgiving. A young Jewish woman who had been attending our services came to faith in Christ, and we baptized her. Soon after she became a Christian, she started facing a barrage of questions from her family. Being so new to the faith, she was having a hard time explaining Christianity to them. Her relatives weren't devout, so they were not threatening any drastic measures over her decision to become a Christian, but they were concerned. One morning after the service, this young lady came to me and asked, "If you had to summarize Christianity in one word, what word would you pick?"

I had to step back and think for a minute. I mean, there were options here. I could have gone with the safe answer and said, "Jesus." I could have said "salvation" or "heaven." I could have thrown her for a loop with "propitiation." I could have said "love." Any of those would have been good answers, but as I thought about it more, I realized that the best word to sum up Christianity is really the word "servant." Christianity is about being a servant. Jesus said to be a servant. Paul went a step beyond servanthood and called himself a slave to Jesus Christ.

I'm convinced that Jesus was keen on creating servants because serving is the ultimate expression of love. After all, a little earlier in Matthew, when someone asks Jesus to pinpoint the greatest command in Scripture, Jesus replies, "'You must love the LORD your God with all your heart, all your soul, and all your mind.' This is the first and greatest commandment. A second is equally important: 'Love your neighbor as yourself'" (Matt. 22:37–39). Love is the greatest commandment, and service is the ultimate outward expression of love. It makes sense then that Jesus said the greatest among us would be servants. Mother Teresa spoke to this truth when she said, "Love cannot remain by itself—it has no meaning. Love has to be put into action, and that action is service."[1] The greatest are those who allow God's love to flow through them most freely in the form of service to the people around them. Which takes us back to date night and Henry . . .

Henry's title was "server." His job was to serve, but he had no interest in being a servant. His motivation was not love but something else altogether. Being a servant is an issue of the heart. Sure, Henry, Joe Churchgoer, you, and I can go through the motions of serving someone, but if love isn't our impetus, our service is empty. If love *is* our motivation, however, we will be translating the gospel through action to the person we are serving. Part of mobilizing people for significant ministry is helping them understand the heart of service. Serving may be a humble position, but it takes a great soul to do it well. And when done well, it leads to light being poured through the kingdom, as the server becomes more like Jesus and those being served begin to see his love.

2

clarifying your theology of ministry

EIGHT BIBLICAL PRINCIPLES
FOR AN EFFECTIVE SYSTEM

I am of the opinion that my life belongs to the community, and as long as I live, it is my privilege to do for it whatever I can. I want to be thoroughly used up when I die, for the harder I work, the more I live.

—George Bernard Shaw

For even the Son of Man came not to be served but to serve others and to give his life as a ransom for many.

—Jesus (Matthew 20:28)

When I was just starting in ministry, one of my most re-spected mentors said something to me that I've never forgotten. As I was venting to him about feeling like a one-man show in my young church, much like David to Tim (but perhaps with a bit more frustration), he put his arm around me and said, "Nelson, remember, every member in your church is a minister. You are not in this alone unless you choose to be."

Every member is a minister. I'm sure you've heard that assertion time and time again. It may even be one of the core values of your church. Honestly, when I first heard the statement, I wasn't sure what it meant. But now, after decades in ministry and countless hours spent working with pastors around the world, I realize just how deep this truth runs and how important it is when you are working to lead a God-honoring, effective church. In fact, I've taken the concept a step further. Around The Journey, we believe that every attender is a minister, whether they have taken the step of membership or not, but more on that later.

The belief that "every member is a minister" is something that most of us hold as a basic tenet of our theology of ministry—even if we don't realize we have a theology of ministry in place. Our problem lies in that lack of realization. You and I, as leaders in God's kingdom, cannot afford to have a weak, clichéd, or underdeveloped theology of ministry. Sure, we may believe that every member is a minister, but if we haven't worked through the associated *why* and *how* of that belief, we will have a hard time fleshing out its reality. Before you can start implementing the ministry system and increasing your number of volunteers, you have to take the foundational step of clarifying your theology of ministry; you have to make sure that the assumptions you are working with about service are built on prayerful study of the New Testament rather than on old tradition.

A proper theology of ministry will rapidly expand your ministry system, while a small theology of ministry will constrain it. The theology you adhere to will determine your convictions and the confidence with which you call people to serve. In other words, once you have a strong theology of ministry in place, you will have deeper assurance and more passion about the details of ministry in your church. You will be more likely to invite people to take action steps of faith, and you will be able to do so with increased confidence.

> *A proper theology of ministry will rapidly expand your ministry system, while a small theology of ministry will constrain it.*

After a slightly longer wait than usual, the waiter reappears with Tim's and David's breakfast. The two take advantage of the lag time to chitchat about the upcoming playoffs. Tim hasn't brought David's comments about being a one-man show back up yet. But once their food is situated, he decides not to let David's words linger any longer. Capping the blueberry syrup and cutting into his pancakes, Tim says, "David, let me ask you a question. Have you really thought about *why* people serve at your church?"

"Well, sure," David answers. "Some of them just want to. I guess they know serving is good for them . . . and there are so many things that need to be done every week that their serving is good for me too!" David chuckles as he takes a bite of his toast.

"Yeah, but the real reason your people need to be connected in serving runs deeper. Not to sound preachy, but the truth is, when people serve, they become more like Jesus. When you encourage them to serve and then do what it takes to get them involved, you are discipling them—which is your role as their pastor. It's not just so things at the church get done," Tim says.

"I hear you, Tim. I do." David wipes his mouth with his napkin and leans back in the booth for a minute. "Honestly, I'm really not sure what to do to get more people involved. I feel like there are all of these needs, but I don't want to impose on anyone. I mean, I do understand that serving is biblical and that I am not actually asking them for my own benefit, but it still feels that way sometimes."

Tim puts his fork down, leans in, and looks David in the eye. "Listen, David. I am giving you permission, right now, to ask your people to serve. You aren't supposed to be a one-man show. God wants your people involved in building up his church, and he has put you in a position to make sure that happens. If you keep hesitating, you won't only be hurting yourself; you'll be hurting all of your people. Believe me, I learned this lesson the hard way."

Tim sits back and takes a sip of his coffee, then continues, "The first thing you have to do, though, is make sure you know what you believe about serving."

"What do you mean?"

"I mean, you have to nail down your theology of ministry. Do you have a piece of paper handy?"

David pulls a notebook out of his bag, hands Tim a pen, and leans in, eager to learn what it takes to put an end to his constant volunteer shortage.

At The Journey, we have built our theology of ministry around eight theological foundations. Now you don't have to adopt our theology of ministry carte blanche, but here's what I do ask of you: use these eight principles to help you think critically about how and why people serve in your church. As you work through each one, let it spur you toward clarifying your own theology of ministry, so you can move forward with building your ministry system on a proper foundation.

Foundation 1: Ministry means to serve.

We often confuse people with our language. When your members hear you say that you want them to get involved in ministry, they don't understand what that really means. The word *ministry* causes them to tailspin into thoughts like, "Ministry? Oh, I'm not qualified. I would have to go through a bunch of training or get ordained or something. . . . I can't commit to that." You and I understand that we are simply asking our people to volunteer. We are calling them to engage the gifts and abilities God has given them by serving Jesus through the local church. Make sure your members understand that being involved in ministry doesn't mean they have to go to seminary or join the staff. Ministry simply means to serve.

Foundation 2: Serving is the act of putting the needs of others before our own needs.

Serving is an expression of selflessness. Unfortunately, our modern cultural mindset is one of wanting to be served rather than serving—and that's as true in our churches as anywhere else. In fact, I believe that selfishness is one of the greatest sins we face in today's church. Everyone wants to be served; few are interested in serving. Even those who are willing to volunteer often let selfishness creep into their service. You've seen it: people who become overly comfortable in *their* position and are unwilling to give anyone else an opportunity; or servers who will do their job willingly, but have no interest in bolstering the kingdom by training others.

Selfishness, which does nothing but foster the status quo, is comfortable. Putting others' needs first can be awkward and messy. But just as you and I have been called to serve selflessly, so have each and every one of our people. We have a duty to lead them toward the life of service that Jesus emulated. As he says in Matthew 20:28, "For even the Son of Man came not to be served but to serve others."

Foundation 3: The goal of the ministry system is to help people become like Jesus.

As church leaders, you and I are responsible for helping our people become more and more like Jesus. That's God's goal for every individual he has placed under your care. As Paul wrote to the early Christians in Rome,

> For God knew his people in advance, and he chose them to become like his Son, so that his Son would be the firstborn among many brothers and sisters. And having chosen them, he called them to come to him. And having called them, he gave them right standing with himself. And having given them right standing, he gave them his glory. (Rom. 8:29–30)

God chose each one of us and called us to himself so that we would become like his Son. That's the ultimate goal. So, as you begin to think about developing an effective ministry system and doubling your volunteer base, the real question isn't "How many more volunteers can I have?" but rather "How many of my people are more like Jesus because they are connected in serving?"

Foundation 4: You cannot become like Jesus Christ unless you learn to be a servant.

Helping people learn to be servants, then, is an essential part of discipleship. In order to strip away selfishness and move people toward being servants, we need to model servanthood, teach on servanthood, and challenge volunteers onward as we celebrate and reproduce the Christlike characteristics in their lives. We'll discuss all of this in much more detail in the pages ahead. For now, just remember: serving is essential to becoming like Jesus.

Foundation 5: Serving opens people's hearts to God and therefore is part of worship.

This foundation has profound implications for both Christians and non-Christians. Before an unbeliever can come to know Jesus and worship him in truth, God has to open his heart to the reality of the gospel. In my experience, non-Christians who find themselves in serving situations become receptive to God's work in their life much more readily than those who don't serve. Here's my theory: The portion of a

45

person's heart that is closed to God is guarded by a door that swings on the hinges of service. When someone starts serving others, the hinges loosen up and that closed door begins to swing open.

For Christians, service not only opens people's hearts to worship but also stands as an act of worship in and of itself. When we present our bodies and our time to God as willing servants, we are worshiping him. Take a look at another piece of Paul's letter to the Roman church:

> And so, dear brothers and sisters, I plead with you to give your bodies to God because of all he has done for you. Let them be a living and holy sacrifice—the kind he will find acceptable. This is truly the way to worship him. (Rom. 12:1)

Believers who give themselves to God through service, as an act of worship, are essentially pouring themselves out for the benefit of others. They are putting the needs of someone else before their own needs. Then, when these servants approach God in their quiet time or in corporate worship, he finds their sacrifice acceptable and is faithful to refill them—so they can go and pour themselves out again.

Too often you and I are hesitant to call people to ministry because we think the request will be seen as self-serving. We fall into feeling like we are trying to recruit people for our own purposes. Such thinking is completely off base. If your vision is aligned with God's purposes for your church, asking people to get involved with that vision is asking them to start doing the most important thing they can do in life. You are calling them to an act of worship.

Foundation 6: If people aren't serving, they aren't truly worshiping and growing in their faith.

Given this theological foundation, serving is a good way to measure worship and growth in your church. Let's get practical here. You can use serving to measure how deeply people are worshiping and how much they are growing by implementing the 30/50/20 Rule. Studies have shown that growth in most churches correlates with the number of people serving. In the majority of churches, the numbers aren't great. Typically, 95 percent of the people are sitting, soaking, and souring while 5 percent are serving. Have you ever pastored that church? I know I have.

One of my favorite images of ministry is the football game analogy. Go to any college or professional football game and you'll see twenty-two people on the field who are in desperate need of rest and tens of thousands of people in the stands who are in desperate need of exercise. Too often, that's how our churches look. We have lots of people sitting on the sidelines who desperately need to grow, while the small minority who does everything desperately needs to take a break. That game plan may work in sports, but it will hinder your church in terms of both spiritual and numerical growth.

The Pareto principle, also known fittingly as "The Law of the Vital Few," holds that approximately 80 percent of all results come from 20 percent of causation factors. In our language, this principle would equate to 80 percent of the ministry being done by 20 percent of the people. Sadly, in most churches, the percentage of involvement is much lower—which is why, I suppose, all of the books I've ever read on ministry contend that getting the Pareto principle going in our churches would be an impressive feat; they think that having 20 percent of churchgoers doing 80 percent of the work would be a good thing. I don't agree; I believe God has more in store for our people and his church. The Pareto principle, while it has its place in many areas of economic thought, shouldn't apply to our ministry efforts. God's plan is for far more than 20 percent of his children to be actively involved in his work. Let's challenge such limited thinking and take on God's point of view instead.

To that end, here's how the 30/50/20 Rule works: At any given time, I want 30 percent of our church to be sitting on the sidelines. I think of them as pre-servers. There's never been a week where we missed that goal, as you can imagine— sometimes we greatly surpass it! Next, I want 50 percent of our church serving one hour per week. They may be leading a growth group, singing on the worship team, serving as an usher or greeter, working in the kids' area, or whatever else they are best suited to do. The point is that they are involved in serving in some way for an hour each week. As the church grows, the number of active servers expands accordingly. If you consistently hit that 50 percent mark, you will never be lacking for volunteers.

The 20 percent part of the measurement doesn't directly concern the ministry system. Briefly, I want to have 20 percent of the church involved in some kind of evangelism or outreach ministry. For example, they may invite a friend to church or take part in a formal evangelism project or event. That may not be where you want to focus the last 20 percent. Feel free to modify the measurement in the way that best fits your church.

We've talked about how the church is a body, made up of systems. Well, the 30/50/20 Rule provides you with an accurate snapshot of your pulse and blood pressure combined. If you are hitting close to the 30/50/20 mark, you have a healthy heart rate. Maybe right now, your equation looks more like 85/10/5. Start working to move those numbers in the direction you want them to go. Your first goal may be to change your current equation to 65/20/15. The important thing is to figure out where you are, and then set your benchmarks and work toward them.

Foundation 7: Mobilizing people for ministry is part of discipleship.

If someone in your church is not serving, he is not growing as a disciple. If he isn't serving, he's less likely to be sharing his faith, spending time in Scripture and in prayer, and giving in a God-honoring way. In short, if he isn't serving, he is not going to be able to honor God with all of the other areas of his life. Your job and mine, as church leaders, is to disciple people. We are called to help them down the path of offering their whole lives to God. Mobilizing them for ministry is an indispensable part of that discipleship.

Foundation 8: The role of the pastor is to equip people for ministry.

As a pastor, if I am doing everything by myself, I am robbing the people in my church of opportunities to grow. Having a do-it-yourself attitude is dangerous when it comes to ministry. (We'll discuss this in much greater detail a little later.) It's in my best interest not only as a pastor but also as a kingdom builder to mobilize as many people as possible to be involved in ministry. I am called to equip them. As Paul says in Ephesians 4:11–13,

> Now these are the gifts Christ gave to the church: the apostles, the prophets, the evangelists, and the pastors and teachers. Their responsibility is to equip God's people to do his work and build up the church, the body of Christ. This will continue until we all come to such unity in our faith and knowledge of God's Son that we will be mature in the Lord, measuring up to the full and complete standard of Christ.

Our responsibility is not to be a one-person show; our responsibility is to equip people to do God's work and to build up his church in doing so. (For a free downloadable and editable copy of our Eight Foundations, visit www. ChurchLeaderInsights.com/connect.)

Clarifying Questions

Now that you understand the significance of clarifying your theology of ministry, spend some time examining your theology before you move on. Take a few minutes, alone or with your team, to think through the questions below. These questions, combined with what you have just learned and with your own prayer and study, will help you begin developing a theology of ministry that will honor God and shepherd your people well. (For a free download of this theology of ministry questionnaire to use with your team, visit www. ChurchLeaderInsights.com/connect.)

1. How am I becoming more like Jesus?

2. How are the leaders in my church modeling Christlike servanthood?

3. How is serving others part of following Jesus Christ?

4. What are the key Scriptures that will define beliefs about ministry in our church?

5. Are there positions in my church where non-Christians can serve?

_____

_____

_____

_____

_____

6. When was the last time I did a theological study of ministry? How have my views changed/deepened?

_____

_____

_____

_____

_____

creating
opportunity

3

a first step into service

GENERATING POINTS OF ENTRY

The first step, my son, which one makes in the world, is the one upon which depends the rest of our days.

—Voltaire

God has given each of you a gift from his great variety of spiritual gifts. Use them well to serve one another.

—1 Peter 4:10

A few years ago we had a high-powered investment broker in our church. This guy, Stuart, was as sharp as they come. Stuart was smart and engaging. He lived in a beautiful apartment on the Upper West Side of Manhattan. He traveled internationally for work, stayed in five-star hotels, and dined with the CEOs and CFOs of major corporations. Still, whenever Stuart was in town on a Thursday night, he would show up at The Journey offices for our Super Service Thursday—a time when volunteers come in for an hour to fold and stuff programs and take care of other tasks in preparation for the upcoming Sunday.

During the time when Stuart was around (he has since moved to Tokyo), we hired a new, young staff pastor. After a few weeks on the job, this pastor commented to me that he was a little surprised Stuart was so faithful in coming to Super Service Thursday. He thought someone like Stuart must have better things to do with his time than chitchat and slide inserts into programs.

One Thursday night, this young pastor struck up a conversation with Stuart, during which he thanked Stuart for being there. Stuart replied with something that shifted the way our new pastor looked at serving. He said, "Oh, I would hate to miss it. This hour on Thursday night is the only time I feel like I am doing something that really matters." Stuart had a glamorous, well-paying dream job, but he understood that his job didn't bring him significance. Rather, serving the church in whatever way he could made him feel like he mattered—like he was making a difference for eternity instead of just making money.

Stepping toward Significance

Here's something I know about Stuart: the first time he took the step to show up at Super Service Thursday, he was nervous. He was out of his comfort zone. He told me later that he was there in response to a sermon series I had taught out of Philippians 2. Even though he hadn't known exactly what he was getting himself into, he had understood the significance of being a servant and had taken a first step to get involved. Thanks to our clarified theology of ministry and the ministry system we have in place, Stuart internalized the imperative to serve and was able to get easily plugged into an area that worked well with his schedule.

First steps are scary. They stretch us and push us out of our comfort zone. But even though they may be uncomfortable, first steps are essential to moving forward into God's best for our lives. Part of the difficulty in recruiting volunteers for ministry is the simple fact that you are pushing against their natural tendency to stay within their comfort zones. You are asking them to expend time and energy—two things they may already feel short on—in order to step into something completely selfless. Or, at least, that's how they could see it if they don't understand the significance of serving. In reality, when you ask people to take a first step into service, you are inviting them into something much bigger than themselves. Once they become involved, they will be glad they did.

This is why clarifying your theology of ministry, as we discussed in the last chapter, is so important. If you aren't convinced of the importance of what you are asking your people to do—both for them personally and for the kingdom of God—you will struggle with inviting them into meaningful ministry. Do you really believe that having someone show up and serve can help him or her mature as a Christian? I hope so. Again, make sure you have worked through and internalized your theology of ministry before moving forward. So much depends on it. (If you still aren't sure that you understand your theology of ministry, I encourage you to revisit chapter 2 before continuing.)

Once your theology of ministry is nailed down, you can begin mobilizing new servers like Stuart for first-time service opportunities in two ways. The first way is to increase the number of new people in your *current* ministry positions. In other words, create a strategy for getting new people involved in your existing areas of ministry. The second way to mobilize new servers is to recruit people to *new* ministry positions. We'll talk about the former in this chapter and the latter in chapter 4.

> **Two Ways to Mobilize New Servers**
>
> 1. Increase the number of new people in *current* ministry positions.
> 2. Recruit new people to *new* ministry positions.

Mobilizing People for Current Ministry Opportunities

Think through the current ministries operating in your church. You probably have a children's ministry, a worship arts ministry, a small groups ministry, an ushering/greeting ministry, and several other areas where volunteers are actively involved and vitally important. The first way you can begin to mobilize new servers is by creating first-serve opportunities in these existing areas. Here's how:

Encourage the involvement of new people by always putting a time limit on serving. In other words, never allow anyone to step into a ministry position without putting time boundaries on his service. If you provide no time limits, two things will happen:

1. Your volunteers will burn out.
2. You will lose invaluable opportunities to mobilize new servers.

Let's examine this through the lens of small group volunteers. At The Journey, our small groups run on a semester-based calendar, with three semesters each year. When someone becomes a group leader, we let him know that he can only lead two of the three semesters in any given year. Once he serves as a group leader for two semesters, we want him to take a semester off before leading again. Now, we have people at our church who love to lead groups, as I'm sure you do too. Sometimes they tell us they don't need to take a semester off. Still, we require them to. Why? Because experience has taught us the essential truth of the stress and release principle—that is, people work and grow best when they are actively engaged for a period of time, followed by a period of rest, reflection, and rejuvenation.

I have two brothers, both of whom are professional bodybuilders. They are both several years older than me. Growing up, I was fascinated by these hulk-like demigods who lived in my house. I used to beg to go to the gym with them so I could watch them work out. Sometimes they let me. As I got older, I started noticing the routine of their workouts. They would work their chest one day, their back the next, and their arms on the third day. Then they would start the rotation again. When I asked them why they worked out that way, they told me the number-one rule of bodybuilding: if you put stress on a muscle consistently, it can't grow. Muscles grow during the release period, during the time of rest after the stress.

The same principle applies in ministry. If you allow (or push, but none of us would ever do that, right?) your group leaders to lead continuously, they won't grow like they should or be as valuable to the people they are leading. They'll be so busy on the stress side of things that they won't reap the benefits that come with a release.

In my experience, the leaders who try to tell you that they don't need a break are usually the same ones who will come to you later suffering from burnout. They will eventually get tired; part of our job is to make sure they take a break before they do. Not to mention, every leader needs a period of rest and reflection, while sitting under another leader, in order to be able to operate at full capacity the next time they lead. I often tell people, "We love you too much to let you serve another semester without a break. You need to take some time off and then come back recharged." God was putting this principle to work when he mandated that we observe the Sabbath. We would do well to embrace its power in every area.

More important for our current discussion, the gap created when your leaders take time off allows new leaders to step up to the plate. By putting a time limit on those currently serving, you create new serving opportunities. Does that idea scare you? You may be thinking, "That's all well and good, Nelson, but I need volunteers too badly to take the chance. What if I tell some people they have to take a break from serving and no one steps in to fill their place? I'll be up a creek." Believe me, I can relate. When you first start implementing serving time frames, you may feel like you are taking a major leap of faith. I've been there.

The year we started our small group system at The Journey, I came face-to-face with the initial uneasiness inherent in this idea. As we approached our third semester, I looked around at all of the great group leaders we had—and all of the new leaders we didn't have—and thought that forcing the current leaders to take a break was going to ruin us. I thought I'd never be able to replace them, and that our young groups system would fizzle away as quickly as it had started. Still, I knew that the principle of stress and release was inarguable; I knew that enforcing the time limit on service was a wise thing to do. So I took a few deep breaths, spent a lot of time praying, and bit the bullet.

To my joy and surprise, the current group leaders rose to the occasion and helped find new leaders to lead during that third semester. New volunteers got involved at every level, which bolstered our group system exponentially in the months and years to come. Looking back, building the principle of stress and release into our system from the very beginning was one of the healthiest decisions we ever made. (For more information on The Journey's semester-based small group system, visit www.ChurchLeaderInsights.com/connect and see my previous book *Activate: An Entirely New Approach to Small Groups* [Regal, 2008].)

Divide all existing ministry areas into quads. Another way to give new people first-serve opportunities within existing ministries is to examine every volunteer area in your church and think about how you can divide the responsibilities of that area into four separate sections. Then invite people to serve within each of those sections. Let me explain with an illustration.

Awhile back I was consulting with a church in Georgia that had a weekly attendance of about seven hundred people. They were in a portable situation, so they had to set up and tear down for their service every Sunday. One day, when I was in town, meeting with the church's pastors, one of the guys started telling me about Earl. Earl was an older fellow in the church who had been a volunteer for quite a while. He had one job he wanted to do; he was the sign man. Every Sunday Earl would make sure that the sign made it from storage to its rightful place on the corner of the lot.

Despite his zeal over the church sign, Earl was something of a curmudgeonly old guy who was hard to deal with. The pastors wanted to relieve him of his duties, but they didn't want to hurt his feelings. After all, he had been around forever. So, together, we decided to address the situation—and get new people involved—by dividing Earl's volunteer area into quads, or four separate duties: (1) Get the sign out of the storage unit. (2) Place the sign on the corner of the lot. (3) Take the sign down after church. (4) Wash the sign when needed, and make sure it was kept in good repair.

The next day we sat Earl down and explained to him that he needed to train people to do all four of these things, in case he was sick one Sunday or got unavoidably tied up. We gave him ownership of this new step by getting him involved in finding the people to help him. We knew that Earl wanted to continue placing the sign—that's what he loved to do—so we asked him to find someone who could go get the sign out of storage and meet him at the corner. We asked him who he knew that could take the sign down, and who else might want to handle its cleaning and maintenance.

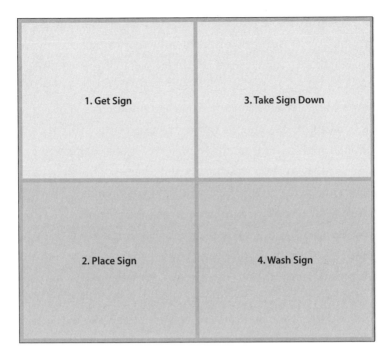

After a few weeks, there was an official sign team. New people were involved, doing everything except placing the sign.

While Earl's story is a simple illustration, it's a model you can follow in every volunteer area of your church. Examine every area and divide them into four smaller areas. Then, find people to serve in each of those smaller areas. This is a simple way to create new volunteer positions within your current ministries.

Create A-B-C teams for each ministry area. As Three Dog Night sang in the 1960s, "One is the loneliest number." If you have only one team in place for each ministry area of your church—i.e., one worship team, one children's ministry team, one ushering team, etc.—you will eventually find yourself in trouble. What if several of the members of that one team are unavailable on the same day? What if some of the volunteers need to take a break at the same time? Would you be left scrambling? What ministry would go undone?

Creating A-B-C teams not only ensures that you always have enough people available to serve; it also helps you get significantly more people involved in every volunteer area in your church. In essence, you multiply your teams by having more than one team in place for any given ministry. Then you set up a schedule of rotation for those teams. When you have A-B-C teams in place, no team is ever full, so there are always opportunities to involve new servers.

For example, say a member of your church, Julie, comes to you and says that she'd like to be part of the worship team. The only problem is that your worship team is packed with people who want to serve. A-B-C teams solve the problem by opening up the opportunity for Julie and other potential volunteers to get involved. Not to mention, they allow your current worship team volunteers to rest, and they give you assurance that you will never be short on volunteers in that area. Here's how it works:

You create three worship teams—worship team A, worship team B, and worship team C. Each team is made up of people who are eager and qualified to be part of leading worship during a weekend service. Then, you simply create a schedule that your three worship teams rotate through. For instance, schedule worship team A to lead for a month, and then they take a break while worship team B leads for a month. Then worship team C leads for a month, and you start the rotation over again. Or you could have the three teams alternate by weeks, or by quarters. You get the picture.

With A-B-C teams, you have the flexibility to schedule your service rotations in whatever way works best for your culture. The point is that no team serves for more than a few months. The rotation will make sure everyone is practicing the principle of stress and release, and it will continually open doors for new people to get involved in existing ministries. A-B-C teams can work for any ministry, from the worship team to the ushering team to Earl's sign team. All you are doing is multiplying ministries and thereby multiplying ministers.

I can almost hear you thinking, "I have a hard time filling up one team, much less finding enough people for three!" Let me challenge you to let go of that scarcity mentality. God has droves of people whom he wants to plug into your ministries—for your church's benefit and for their own. Let's not let our limited thinking limit his plans. The principle of spiritual readiness says we must prepare and plan for the harvest before God will send it to us. Choose to believe that you can have A-B-C teams in every ministry area of your church. Allow yourself to begin imagining what that would look like. Then keep reading. Internalize and begin working the system in these pages. You'll be amazed at how God will use it for his glory.

Plan a shadow day. Put a shadow day on your calendar, and invite every person who is currently serving to bring a friend to shadow them that day. The goal here is that the friends who show up will enjoy serving and want to do it again. Whether they want to ultimately serve in the same capacity as the friend they shadowed is irrelevant. The shadow day simply gets them into a service setting and gives them a taste of what it's like to be involved.

An added bonus of the shadow day is that you will have at least one other person familiar with every ministry position. Again, one is a lonely number; in my opinion, it's a really bad number for anything except a spouse. Options are not optional when it comes to ministry, so you've got to have different people who know how to do what needs to be done at every level. If all of your servers bring a friend to shadow them for a day, then you've doubled the number of in-the-know volunteers at your church. Even if these new people don't get involved right away, you may be able to call on them in a pinch.

Hold a ministry/volunteer fair. Once a year, hold a ministry fair to make people aware of all of the serving opportunities available to them. While they are neither new nor novel, ministry fairs can be effective. When you do your fair, take special care to:

1. Make sure the details of each ministry position are crystal clear. People will rarely sign up for something they don't understand.
2. Make sure the sign-up process is simple. A complicated sign-up process is nothing but a stumbling block to getting people involved. (We'll go into more detail on the sign-up process in chapter 5.)

Use big days and special events to challenge people to serve. Never waste an opportunity to get new people involved in ministry. Leverage every big event and special occasion. Many of the people in your church who aren't currently serving would be more willing to serve on a big day or for a special event than for a normal weekend service. So, when anything out of the ordinary is happening, invite new people to be a part of it through serving.

Several years ago, The Journey was meeting at a performance center in midtown Manhattan. The venue had two main theaters, an upstairs theater and a downstairs theater, and we usually met upstairs. Every once in a while, though, the venue would book something upstairs on a Sunday and we would have to meet in the downstairs theater instead. Technically, this wasn't a big deal for us. In some ways it was easier to set up downstairs than upstairs. But every time the venue asked us to move downstairs for a week, I leveraged the opportunity to try to get new people to serve.

I would send an email to people in our church who weren't currently involved in serving and say, "Hey, we just found out that this Sunday we are going to have to move our service to the downstairs theater. This would be a perfect opportunity for you to come early and help out, because it's going to take more volunteers than ever to make sure we have a great experience in the downstairs theater." I took the opportunity to create a sense of urgency, and you know what? New people would sign up to serve. Once they were there, we made sure they enjoyed serving, earnestly thanked them for their time, and asked them to do it again.

When you give potential servers an immediate "why," they will often respond. People get involved when they have a specific reason to get involved. Otherwise, they may want to get involved, but they can continually justify putting it off until next month, next quarter, or next year. Always ask yourself, "What are we doing this week that could get more people involved in serving than last week?" and then invite new people to serve.

Use people from the last membership class or baptism to serve at the next membership class or baptism. When you have a membership class, baptism, or other similar event coming up, reach out to your new, potential servers who were involved in the last generation of that event. This is an excellent first-step service opportunity. The goal is to have new servers take a first step by involving them in an area close to their hearts and then move them toward serving again and again.

For example, if Joe Newbeliever was baptized in January, ask him to serve at the baptism you are doing in May. Since he enjoyed his baptism experience, he will likely be eager to make sure the people being baptized this time enjoy theirs. Then, when May's baptism celebration is wrapping up, pull Joe (and the other new volunteers) aside, thank him for his willingness to serve, and ask him to sign up to serve at a weekend service. Simply say something along the lines of, "Hey Joe, I can tell you enjoyed serving today, I bet you would really enjoy being a greeter on Sunday. How about we go ahead and sign you up for a Sunday later this month?"

At The Journey, our membership class is completely facilitated by volunteers who were participants in the previous membership class. Outside of the pastor who is leading the class, they are running things. They handle the check-in, pass out the papers, take a picture of the new members, and do whatever else needs to be done. Since these servers are new members who have recently gone through the class themselves, they are excited to serve. When the membership class wraps up, we thank them for serving, remind them that the church runs through the faithful service of volunteers, and get them involved in serving at a weekend service.

Taking the Fear Away

Many of the potential volunteers in your church are sitting on the sidelines out of fear. They are hesitant to get involved because they don't know what their involvement will look like. They're afraid they'll get stuck doing something that they are uncomfortable with or that will take too much of their time. Or maybe they volunteered somewhere else in the past and had a bad experience, so they are subconsciously self-protecting.

By being intentional about opening new positions in current ministries through putting time limits on serving, dividing jobs into smaller tasks, guarding against burnout, and allowing people to shadow before they serve, you can put your new servers at ease. By holding ministry fairs to answer their questions and help them find the right place to serve, you can assuage some of that fear. And by challenging them through big days and special events, and inviting them to serve in areas close to their hearts, you can encourage them to take that first step in a way that will feel natural and exciting.

Peter reminds us in 1 Peter 4:10 that each of us has been given a spiritual gift to serve one another. If our attenders and members aren't willing and able to take the first step into ministry by getting involved in current ministry opportunities, we aren't doing our part to shepherd them into servanthood. We'll dive much deeper into the discussion on identifying specific gifts and matching those with specific areas of service a little later. For now, let's continue to focus on helping them take that first step, as it's the most important step in the journey ahead.

4

the power
of new beginnings

RECRUITING NEW PEOPLE FOR MINISTRY

Start by doing what's necessary; then do what's possible; and
suddenly you are doing the impossible.

—St. Francis of Assisi

For I am about to do something new.
See, I have already begun! Do you not see it?
I will make a pathway through the wilderness.
I will create rivers in the dry wasteland.

—Isaiah 43:19

Getting new people involved in current ministry positions is
crucial to increasing your volunteer base, but it's only one

piece of the puzzle. Every great leader knows that being able to see the need for something new in your organization and acting to address that need is key to continued forward momentum. Visionary leaders see the potential problems and opportunities that are coming down the pike long before they arrive, and then they take the initiative to prepare for them, capture them, and leverage them well. These leaders take the words of the famous motivational author Robert Collier to heart: "As fast as each opportunity presents itself, use it! No matter how tiny an opportunity it may be, use it!"[2] When it comes to mobilizing more volunteers in your church, the same thinking applies. When an opportunity presents itself, use it!

Mobilizing People for New Ministry Opportunities

In the last chapter we discussed how to get new people involved in current ministry positions. The second way to mobilize people for ministry is to create first-serve opportunities within new ministry positions. The first step in doing this is to identify specific underserved needs in your church. I call this the "blanks on a page" strategy. Knowing you need to get more people involved in serving, both for their own growth and for God's glory, start thinking about where you would like new people to serve. Where is there a need that's not being met effectively? Where is there an opportunity to create something fresh and exciting? Examine these areas and weigh their potential as new ministry positions.

This is exactly how our Super Service Thursday ministry (or you may remember it as Stuart's place of service) began. Back in the day, our staff folded all of our programs for the

Sunday service. As the church began to grow, this way of operating became problematic. Our staff couldn't be responsible for folding so many programs on top of their regular duties. We found ourselves in a position where we either needed to hire a few people to come in and do the job or we needed to start recruiting volunteers to help us get ready for the weekend service. Obviously, we never want to hire someone to fill a gap that could be a serving opportunity for one of our members or attenders. So instead we used the need as a chance to get new people involved in serving.

As with so many areas of ministry, clarity is key when it comes to mobilizing people for new opportunities. What exactly needs to be done? How many people do you need and for how long? Too many churches start recruiting volunteers based on the fact that they need more people serving, but they fail to identify the specifics of that service. As a result, even if new people get involved, they quickly fall away thanks to a lack of direction. Clarity is crucial to establishing new ministry positions and to keeping your new volunteers happy and engaged. To that end, here are two things to do when mobilizing people for a need that you've identified:

1. **Create a onetime opportunity to meet the need.**
Your first step isn't to create a whole new ministry; your first step is to create a onetime opportunity to meet the need you've identified. For example, when we realized that we needed volunteers to help us fold and stuff programs, we initiated a onetime event to get some volunteers involved. We let the church know that we needed four people to come in one evening (not

every week, just one specific evening) to help prepare the programs for the next Sunday. Later in this chapter, you'll see why it's not wise to speak in terms of "needing" volunteers, but for this onetime opportunity, it is what it is. You need people to volunteer.

2. **Personally recruit people to serve.**

Your ability to personally recruit volunteers is one of the most underestimated tools you have in your arsenal. Church leaders would do well to take a lesson from the world of sales. Every good salesperson knows that the first step of a sale is to qualify your prospect. In our world, that means that you have to make sure they have the ability to complete the task. Then you have to clearly outline what's involved in what you are selling and close the sale—or, rather, make the Big Ask.

Recruiting people to serve in new ministry positions requires that you become a master asker. A good master asker says to a potential volunteer, "Wouldn't you like to make a difference in our church by helping us fold and stuff programs?" A bad master asker says, "You wouldn't want to come in and help us out with some things, would you?"

Similarly, a good master asker isn't afraid to keep asking. Just because a potential volunteer has had to turn you down once or twice doesn't mean you should stop asking her to get involved. Keep asking. I learned the power of asking over and over during my high school years. If I called a girl to ask her out on a date and she said no, I would promptly ask her, "Well, is your sister home?" I actually got a few dates that way! Never shy away from the Big Ask.

Cast the Vision for Continuing

Once you have identified a need, created a onetime opportunity to meet the need, and personally recruited people to serve, your next step is to cast the vision for continuing the new ministry.

Back to the program-folding example: we scheduled the onetime event for people to come into our office and help fold and stuff the programs. We decided to hold it on a Thursday night from 5:00 to 7:00. I emailed some members who were not involved in serving. I got on the telephone and called a few people who had expressed an interest in serving but had never really found a place to do so. All in all I connected with about twenty people and let them know I was looking for four people to come to the office on Thursday night to be part of a little "program party." We were planning to put a movie on the projector, provide some finger foods, and give people the chance to fellowship while doing something helpful for the service. Fourteen people showed up for what would become our very first Super Service Thursday.

The question at this point becomes, how do you turn a onetime serving opportunity into a new ongoing ministry like Super Service Thursday? You cast vision for continuing the ministry. For example, when our onetime program-folding event was winding down, I pulled everyone together and talked to them about how powerful it would be if this were to become an ongoing ministry. I cast the vision for a weekly Super Service Thursday that would bring people together for fellowship and give them an opportunity to serve in a meaningful way. As part of casting this vision, I taught everyone the principle of the chain. The principle of the chain says that every volunteer position within the church is a link in the chain of someone coming to faith in Jesus Christ. Take a look at this illustration:

The Principle of the Chain

Every volunteer position within the church is a link in the chain of someone coming to faith in Jesus Christ.

Unchurched Person — Jesus Christ

It is important for your volunteers to understand that their service—no matter how big or small—is an integral part of a much bigger picture. The danger I foresaw with Super Service Thursday is that the people who volunteered might not see how folding and stuffing programs was really impacting the kingdom. So, harkening back to the importance of clarity, I talked to them about their link on the chain. I made sure they thought about the fact that the programs they had just folded would go into the hands of people who needed to know Jesus; the message notes they stuffed would give people a place to write down truths that could change their lives; the connection cards they slid in would give people who may be flying under the radar an opportunity to connect with the church and with their Creator more deeply. Even though these program folders may never teach a message or sing a solo, they play an important part in leading people down the path of salvation.

The principle of the chain is something to go back to time and time again. It's not enough to remind your people how significant their service is just once or twice; tell them frequently. Make sure new people hear it. Make sure people who have been serving for years hear it again. Your volunteers stay engaged when they understand the impact of what they are doing. This goes for every area of your church. The workers in your children's ministry need to be reminded that their service is giving new people a chance to hear the gospel. Every week we make sure the worship team volunteers know how many people accepted Jesus—they played a big part in creating that environment. The principle of the chain is a reality every volunteer needs to have ingrained in his or her heart.

Now that you have cast the vision for turning your onetime event into an ongoing ministry, you can move ahead with recruiting regular volunteers. As you invite new people to serve in this ministry, remember the importance of creating a specific serving timeframe for the new positions. In other words, when you ask someone to serve, define how long he'll be serving. Creating a specific serving timeframe is part of establishing and maintaining clarity within your new ministry positions. Knowing that they aren't going to be responsible for serving in a certain position from now until Jesus comes back will make your potential server much more likely to respond positively. Not to mention, the timeframe gives you a natural ending point if things aren't working out for some reason. Your new servers can always choose to continue with the service, but never let them start painting without establishing the borders of the canvas, so to speak.

Need and Belonging

Our thoughts shape the world around us, don't you agree? As the English poet John Milton famously said, "We see things not as they are but as we are."[3] Keep this in mind as you move forward with building your volunteer base—especially when it comes to your mindset about issues of *need and belonging*. Regarding need, I'd like you to eliminate that concept from your mind—and the word from your ministry vocabulary— completely. Never think in terms of need. As for belonging, well, I invite you to wrestle with the contrarian idea that your volunteers may not need to believe before you invite them to belong. The way you think about these two areas will have significant ramifications for your ministry system. Let's dig a little deeper.

The Four-Letter Word of Ministry

"Need" is a nasty four-letter word when it comes to recruiting volunteers. When you tell your people that you need volunteers in a certain area, what they hear is that you haven't done a thorough job of preparation and stewardship.

Imagine that you are a new attender at a vibrant church. You've just dropped your young daughter off in the children's area and you are settling in for the worship service, when the pastor steps up and makes an announcement that the church needs volunteers for the children's ministry. Suddenly you feel like you've left your child in an understaffed area, which causes you to lose confidence in the church and its ministries. That's definitely not the message you want to convey. In *Simply Strategic Volunteers: Empowering People for Ministry*, Tony Morgan writes, "Preparation communicates value and importance."[4] Need indicates a lack of preparation and subsequently a lack of value and importance.

You never need a volunteer; you have an opportunity for someone to serve.

Need also conveys negativity to your potential servers. No one wants to jump on board a sinking ship. They would rather get involved in thriving areas of opportunity. Your mindset and the language you choose to reflect it are more important that you realize. Instead of operating and speaking out of a scarcity mentality, choose a different lens. Reshape your thinking like this: you never need a volunteer; you have an opportunity for someone to serve.

For example, if we were trying to recruit more people for Super Service Thursday, we would say something along the lines of:

> We have a great opportunity for some of you who really love God and want to use your gifts of administration and organization to come out on Thursday night and be a part of what we call Super Service Thursday, one of the most exciting nights in our church. We get together, watch movies, have some food, and, most importantly, we prepare the materials that we are going to use on Sunday to help people grow in their faith and come to Christ. Why don't you try it for a week? To learn more or to join us, check the box on your connection card.

As a potential server, would you react more positively to that invitation or to, "We need a few people to come by the church office from 5:00 to 7:00 on Thursday and help the staff fold and stuff programs"? Remember, be a master asker. Choose your words wisely.

Belong before Believing

One question I often hear is "Should I allow non-Christians to serve at my church?" In my opinion, the answer is a resounding yes—but I realize that may not be a popular position. Traditional thought has always held that people need to come to saving faith in Jesus Christ, and then take the step of church membership, before being able to serve within the church. In other words, a person had to believe, then belong, before taking any other steps on his or her journey of becoming more like Jesus.

I would argue the more biblical view is that a non-Christian can and should start belonging and becoming even before believing. The outward expression of God's work in individual hearts is more fluid than we've traditionally allowed it to be. Take a look at this chart:

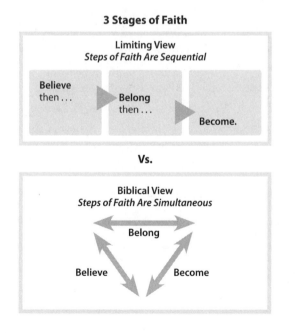

As we touched on previously, the door to an unbeliever's heart often swings on the hinges of service. I've seen this truth play out time and time again. A few years ago I consulted with a church in Florida that held traditional beliefs about serving. Like in most traditional churches, non-Christians were not allowed to volunteer in any capacity. When I came in, the church had recently expanded and was doing well overall, but one of their ministry areas wasn't keeping up with the pace. The parking lot was mayhem every Sunday morning because they had a major shortage of parking lot volunteers. What to do? (As an aside, men love being parking lot greeters. It gives them the chance to play cop. Dentists and lawyers and construction workers—all different types of men—get excited about putting on a reflective vest, grabbing a walkie-talkie, and directing cars toward parking spots. This simple volunteer position helps a lot of men take ownership in their church. Serving—in any capacity—tends to do that.)

Anyway, this was a young church that attracted a lot of unbelievers and seekers. They had quite a few unchurched men who were regular attenders. So we began to examine the possibility of letting some of those guys serve in the parking lot, alongside the team leader and other key players who were Christians, of course. After a lot of discussion, the church leaders agreed to give it a shot. They took an unprecedented step and opened the parking lot ministry to non-Christians. Several unbelieving men jumped at the chance to get involved.

The leaders never expected what happened next. These non-Christian parking lot volunteers started professing faith in Jesus at an astonishing rate. Many of them had been attending the church for months but had never taken a step of faith. By allowing them to be a part of something bigger than their own concerns and rub shoulders with strong Christian men, their hearts became more open to the gospel message. To this day, that Florida church lets unbelievers serve in their parking lot ministry—and in a few other ministries as well.

Opening your thinking to a more fluid progression of faith may be a big hurdle if you come from a traditional background, but it's an extremely healthy move for your church and for the people in it. That said, the extent to which you let non-Christians serve in your church is completely up to you. The approach will look different for your church than it will for mine or for the church down the street. At The Journey, we invite unbelievers to serve liberally alongside believers—peppered into ministry teams that are made up primarily of Christians—because I am convinced that people often have to start belonging to something before they believe.

The worship team is one of the big ways we involve unchurched people in our services. Our team is primarily made up of unpaid professionals—members and attenders—who want to volunteer their time. But we have a lot of services, and sometimes there's a gap to fill. For example, if we are short a drummer one week, we'll hire a professional drummer. Every once in a while, we will end up hiring someone who really enjoys working with us and wants to stick around as a volunteer. If he volunteers for more than three months without taking any noticeable steps of faith, our worship pastor will have a conversation with him about where he is in his spiritual walk. Time and time again, these volunteers end up coming to faith in Christ. Why? Because they had the opportunity to interact with believers, be involved in our services, and be shepherded by our worship arts pastor—all opportunities they never would have had in a more traditional setup. (For more on how we manage worship teams and craft worship services for life transformation, see my book *Engage: A Guide to Creating Life-Transforming Worship Services* [Baker, 2011]. You can also find more information at www. ChurchLeaderInsights.com/connect.)

You can take that model and multiply it out to every other ministry area in your church. As you explore this new idea, define your nonnegotiable areas. For example, we don't let an unbeliever work directly with kids. She may be able to set up the kids area or clean up after service, but only members who have been screened can interact with the children. Similarly, we allow nonbelievers to serve as ushers and collect the offering, but they can't count the offering. Only trusted members are allowed to be on the counting team. Decide for yourself what you are comfortable with.

Remember, God has never operated solely through those who profess faith in him. He used unbelievers for his purposes throughout Scripture and often revealed himself to them in the process. As you think through the stages of faith, I implore you to stay open-minded. Question your point of view and have the courage to shift it if you see fit. You could greatly increase both your ministry system and your evangelism potential by allowing unchurched people to belong to the church and begin becoming more like Jesus before they believe.

5

igniting involvement

ADDITIONAL WAYS TO MOBILIZE VOLUNTEERS

You must get involved to have an impact.

—Napoleon Hill

The harvest is great, but the workers are few. So pray to the
Lord who is in charge of the harvest; ask him to send more
workers into his fields.

—Jesus (Luke 10:2)

Every human being wants to make an impact with his or
her life. The girl who takes your order at the coffee shop is

looking for meaning. The man you pass on your way into the drugstore wants to know that his life matters. Every person you come into contact with today will be somewhere on the continuum of finding and pursuing purpose. Bill Hybels addresses this "divine desire" to find meaning and effect change in his work *The Volunteer Revolution*.

> The desire to be a world-changer is planted in the heart of every human being, and that desire comes directly from the heart of God. We can suffocate that desire in selfishness, silence it with the chatter of competing demands, or bypass it on the fast track to personal achievement. But it's still there. Whenever we wonder if the daily eight-to-five grind or our round-the-clock parenting tasks are all there is to life, that divine desire nudges us. Whenever we feel restless and unsatisfied, the desire whispers in our soul. Whenever we wonder what a life of real purpose would feel like, the desire calls us to something more.[5]

As you and I know, that purpose is found only through a continually deepening relationship with Jesus. And as we've established, serving is fundamental to helping the people under our care grow their relationship with God while becoming more like his Son. When we can come alongside every individual in our church and help them use their gifts and abilities in a meaningful way, we will be discipling as we are called to disciple. Not to mention, we'll be steering them toward the contribution that they are longing to make in this world. To that end, following are a few more steps you can take to get new volunteers connected in your church, through both current and new ministries.

Preach on ministry and serving.

Do your members and attenders understand the biblical imperative to serve? Do they know that Jesus himself was a servant? Have you taught them what the Scriptures have to say about serving? Part of involving people in service is making sure they understand the *why* behind it. That knowledge, combined with their desire to become involved in something bigger than themselves, leads to obedience.

Plan to teach on servanthood at least three times a year. I suggest scheduling one ministry-oriented message in January, one pre-summer, and one pre-fall. These are the three time periods when people are most likely to take a new step and get involved. In addition, do an entire four- to six-week message series on ministry every three years.

Several years ago I taught an expositional sermon series based on Philippians 2. This series, *Positive Living*, was both popular and extremely effective. I'm convinced that it set us on our current path with serving. Throughout the series I called people to step outside themselves and pour their energy into serving others. Every week we offered new serving opportunities and invited people to get involved. We held a big ministry fair on the final Sunday, so everyone could see the full scope of ministry at The Journey. Those six weeks of intentional teaching on the need to become a servant resonated with our people, causing countless numbers to step out of their comfort zones and into significance. Never underestimate the power of preaching on service. (For more information on the *Positive Living* sermon series and how I plan my preaching to connect people into places of services, visit www.ChurchLeaderInsights.com/connect.)

Tie serving to membership and to small groups, and hold people accountable.

Many churches have a membership covenant and a small group covenant in place—a document that people sign when they join the church or a small group. If you don't, I highly recommend making use of two such covenants. Covenants create clarity. They let your people know what is expected of them and give you the ability to hold them accountable to those expectations. Take a look at our membership covenant and small group covenant.

Membership Covenant

- I will protect the unity of my church.
  . . . by acting in love toward other members
  . . . by refusing to gossip
  . . . by following the leaders
- I will share the responsibility of my church.
  . . . by praying for its growth
  . . . by inviting the unchurched to attend
  . . . by warmly welcoming those who visit
- I will serve the ministry of my church.
  . . . by discovering my gifts and talents
  . . . by being equipped to serve by my pastors
  . . . by developing a servant's heart
- I will support the testimony of my church.
  . . . by attending faithfully
  . . . by living a godly life
  . . . by giving regularly

Signature _____

Date _____

The Journey

THE JOURNEY
Growth Group Covenant

Welcome to Growth Groups at The Journey. Congratulations on your desire to grow deeper in your relationship with God through this weekly study and the relationships that will begin in this Growth Group.

As a member of this group, you will be asked to enter into a covenant with the other members to make this Growth Group a priority. To be a part of the group, you are asked to make the following commitments:

1. I will make this group a priority by attending each week, keeping up with my assignments, and participating in group discussion.

2. I will regularly attend The Journey services and contribute to the ministry of the church through my attendance, giving, service, and inviting of others.

3. I will strive to build authentic relationships with those in this group by showing care, providing encouragement, and praying for their needs.

4. I will serve together with my group once a month during the semester and will participate in a mission project and play together with my group at least once.

I will explore honestly my next steps for spiritual growth.

_____   _____
Name   Date

Notice that both the membership covenant and the group covenant call people to serve. Since every member and small group participant has signed at least one of the above

covenants (most have signed both), they are each accountable for what that covenant contains. If we notice that one of
our members has never served, or has become uninvolved in
serving for a substantial period of time, we give them a call
to make sure everything is okay. We can use that call to steer
them back into ministry. (For free editable downloads of both
covenants, visit www.ChurchLeaderInsights.com/connect.)

Small groups are a phenomenal way for people to take a
first step into serving. As you see in the small group covenant,
all of our group members are required to volunteer with
their group during at least one Sunday service per semester.
In general our people get involved with a group before they
start serving. As a result, approximately 70 percent of our new
servers take their first step into serving thanks to this small
group commitment. While they are serving, we take some
time to talk to them about the significance of serving, sign
them up to serve again, and encourage them to get involved
in serving regularly.

Make it easy for people to sign up to serve.

Avoid placing unnecessary stumbling blocks in the path of
people who want to serve. Signing up should be a simple,
streamlined process. I've been in churches where signing up to
serve seemed harder than filling out tax forms. Keep it simple.
How much information do you really need from someone
who wants to work the refreshment table or volunteer in the
office? A name, address, and valid driver's license should be
sufficient. The one exception to this rule is your children's
ministry. When it comes to screening volunteers to work with

your children, I suggest running a full background check. You need to be extra careful with the people with whom you entrust your attenders' children. In general, though, make signing up easy.

At The Journey, we use a connection card to communicate with everyone who attends our services. (For more about connection cards, see *Fusion: Turning First-Time Guests into Fully-Engaged Members of Your Church* [Regal, 2007].) A section on the back of our connection card gives people the opportunity to sign up to serve at an upcoming service and/or gives them a way to request more information about serving in general. Take a look:

I'm Serving Today!

Name:

Email:

Service Time:

☐ First-Time Server   ☐ Second-Time Server
☐ Regular Server   ☐ Serving with my Growth Group
Leader's name:_____

I Would Like to Serve . . .

October
☐ Oct 30

November
☐ Nov 6   ☐ Nov 13   ☐ Nov 20   ☐ Nov 27

December
☐ Dec 4   ☐ Dec 11   ☐ Dec 18

At the Following Service . . .
☐ 10 am   ☐ 11:30 am   ☐ 1:00 pm   ☐ 6:30 pm

☐ Sign me up for teardown after the service

Sunday, October 23, 2011

*"He leads me in paths of righteousness
for His name's sake."*
Psalm 23:3

Service Value of the Week
Serving allows me to give my BEST to God

First Impressions

What did you notice first?
• A wonderful lady greeted me and showed me all of the
tables, explaining the way the services work.
• Everyone was so friendly!

What did you like best?
I noticed that the greeters were very friendly and really
made me feel comfortable and welcomed.

---

4 Things to Remember
1. Greet everyone warmly.
2. Be in position 25 minutes before and after the service
   begins.
3. HAVE FUN!
4. SMILE :-)

My next step today is to:

☐ Memorize Colossians 4:5.
☐ Arrive one hour early to prepare for guests in my church on:
   ☐ Sunday, September 17
   ☐ Sunday, Septermbe 24
   ☐ Sunday, October 1
   ☐ Sunday, October 8
☐ I pray for and invite 5 people to the influence series Kickoff
   on Sunday October 8.
☐ Sign me up for Journey Growth Group # _____

Send me info about:

☐ Becoming a follower of Jesus.
☐ Baptism.
☐ Growth groups.
☐ Church membership.
☐ Serving @ The Journey.
☐ Servant Evangelism Saturday.
☐ Worship Arts Team.
☐ Journey Kidz.

Comments, prayer requests. _____
_____
_____

Someone who wants to serve simply indicates his or her
preferred service date. Then we follow up to confirm and
make sure we have the volunteer's information. If a potential

---

Church Leader Testimony

The best tool we have found to help people use their abilities for Jesus is our connection card. Anytime we have a big serving opportunity, or a smaller one for that matter, we make sure to make signing up for it an easy, one-step process on the reverse side of our connection card. This allows everyone to have the best opportunity to get involved, even first-time guests when it's an appropriate area they can serve in! Using this method has helped us get more men involved in ministry projects because they know exactly what the project is, what it entails, and how long the commitment is.

Pastor Kevin Hill
Holley Church, Sweet Home, Oregon

---

server just wants to get more information about what it means to serve or has questions about anything ministry related, she can check the "Send me info about: Serving @ The Journey" box and we will get in touch with her quickly, answer her questions, and get her signed up to serve.

Notice there is no application. There is no spiritual gifts assessment. Don't misunderstand—I think spiritual gifts assessments are important and serve a purpose in getting people connected in the right areas eventually (as we'll discuss in part 3), but initially they can get in the way. They are not necessary for getting someone involved for the first time and getting someone excited about going deeper in service.

Ask not "How few do we need?" but rather "How many can we mobilize?"

When it comes to volunteers, the church leader's way of thinking too often goes something like this: "Well, we really need three people to make our children's ministry work. I guess we could get by with two. Lord, please send us two people!" Instead of operating out of that scarcity mentality, why not think in terms of abundance? Forget the four-letter-word "need" and ask yourself how many people you can mobilize.

Think back to the ministry quad technique from chapter 3. If you combine this abundance mentality with quads, watch what happens: you may think you need three people to make your children's area work, but when you quad the ministry you actually have opportunities for many more volunteers. You could recruit two people to work check-in, two people to work as security, three people to work with the children, and three people to do cleanup:

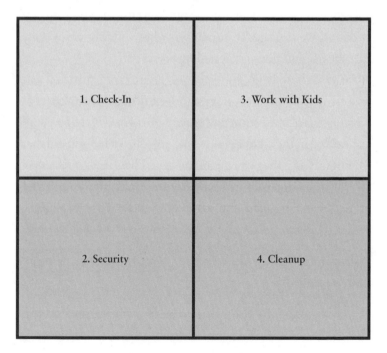

| 1. Check-In | 3. Work with Kids |
| 2. Security | 4. Cleanup |

All of a sudden, there are openings for ten volunteers rather than two. So even if you only recruit seven, you are going to provide a much better experience for the kids and their parents, and you are going to give people who otherwise wouldn't have served an opportunity to get involved. Make this your new volunteer mantra: How many can we mobilize? (Not "How few do we need?")

Never turn away a volunteer.

The unpardonable sin of the ministry system is turning away a volunteer. Many years ago I was sitting in my office at The Journey when I heard an unforgivable conversation take place just outside my door. Apparently, a volunteer had stopped by unannounced, saying she had a couple of hours to help out if there was anything that needed to be done. I almost choked on my coffee when I heard one of our staff people say to her, "Nah, I don't think there's really anything you can do right now." I bolted out of my office to correct the offense. After clarifying to the volunteer that there were significant ways she could contribute, we sat her down at a desk with a bottle of water and told her we'd be right back with her. I conferred privately with my staff person, and we devised a project that would be helpful. Today, if anyone walks through our doors wanting to "help out," we have volunteer-directed projects ready and waiting. And guess what? Now that we are more prepared for them, we have lots of unexpected volunteers show up.

Never, ever, ever turn away someone who wants to serve. You have to build the barn before you can reap the harvest.

Learn from our early close call: at your church's office set up a table that always contains something needing to be sorted or filed, or free up a computer that can access a basic database entry program. Then, when a volunteer unexpectedly shows up at your door to serve, you have something for him to do. Asking him to come back later isn't an option.

Obviously this goes for your weekend services as well. You can never have too many people show up to serve. The more the merrier. If I could, I would have an usher for every single aisle and a trio of greeters at every door, just to get that many people involved. But once again a quick word of warning about your children's ministry: if someone hasn't been properly screened, he shouldn't be allowed to serve in the children's area. Don't let unannounced servers work with kids, but get them passing out programs or helping behind the refreshment table. You can never, ever, ever have too many volunteers.

Tim glances at his watch and signals for the check. "It's unreal how fast the time goes during these breakfasts," he says to David. "I could sit here and talk for hours, but my staff probably wouldn't like that much."

"Yeah, I need to get out of here too," David says. "I have a busy day lined up. But just one more thing, Tim. There's something I'm not clear on. Do you have just a few more minutes?"

"Sure thing. Shoot."

"Okay, so once people start getting involved, how do I make sure they are serving in the right area? I mean, I get the whole idea of clarifying my theology of ministry . . . and I definitely understand creating first-serve opportunities . . . but then what? Do volunteers stay where they start? What about their specific spiritual gifts? How do you make sure they are plugged into—"

"Whoa, slow down." Tim chuckles. "I know exactly what you are asking. Let me give you a little analogy that has always helped me in thinking about ministry. You know the kids' game Chutes and Ladders?"

David lets out a laugh. "Sure do! My daughter wants to play that game just about every night."

"Well, think of your ministry system as Lake and Ladders."

"I'm not sure I follow you . . ." David says.

"There are two parts to your volunteer system. Part 1: get people to take a first step into serving—or jump into the volunteer lake, so to speak. The first time they serve, they are simply jumping in. Maybe they coordinate a small group, or pass out programs at a Sunday service, or serve as an usher. It doesn't matter. The whole point is to get them wet."

"Okay," David says. "I think I see where you are going with this . . ."

Tim gives him a knowing smile. "Then, once these new volunteers have been swimming around in the lake for a little while, part 2: they begin to discern what specific ministry they are suited for—in other words, they decide which ladder they want to climb. Every ministry is its own ladder. Someone who first served at a Sunday service might realize his true calling is to serve on the small group ladder. So he swims over to that ladder and starts climbing. Someone else who first connected through Super Service Thursday might ultimately feel drawn to the worship team. So she swims on over to the worship arts ladder and steps up. Make sense?"

"Yeah, okay, I see," David says. "So it's most important, initially, just to get people connected, in whatever capacity. Then help them find the ministry they are wired for once they are already in the lake."

"Right," Tim confirms. "Otherwise, you are just throwing roadblocks up in their way. If someone wants to serve, let her serve. Let him serve. Anywhere. If they have to figure out exactly where they fit first, they may never get in the lake. And if they never get in the lake . . ."

". . . they are less likely to ever get truly connected," David finishes Tim's sentence. "Lake and Ladders." David chuckles. "I like that." The waiter brings the check over and refills David's coffee.

In *Doing Church as a Team*, Wayne Cordeiro writes,

God would never have given us the great Commission—to go into all the world and preach the gospel—if He never had intended for us to actually move forward. . . . We are called into this great work, but none of us can do it alone. No pastor can single-handedly fulfill such a calling, regardless of how gifted he may be. Unless every one of us catches the fire, in the long run we will lack any warmth against the chill of this present age.[6]

Your job, and mine, is to help our people catch the fire—to do our part to instill in them a burning desire to be involved in God's work. Only when we refuse to do it all ourselves, inspire passion for serving in our people, and mobilize them to serve God through serving his kingdom, will our churches truly be able to move toward the imperative of the Great Commission.

PART 3

cultivating the ministry ladder

6

lake and ladders

HELPING VOLUNTEERS TAKE THE NEXT STEP

God is consistent in his plan for our lives. He would not give each of us inborn abilities, temperaments, talents, spiritual gifts, and life experiences and then not use them!

—Rick Warren

In his grace, God has given us different gifts for doing certain things well.

—Romans 12:6

A friend from my undergraduate days recently had an interesting experience with his seven-year-old son, Danny. Danny is a huge baseball fan in general, but his love for the New York Yankees is something special. He has a life-sized cutout of

Derek Jeter hanging on his bedroom wall. He begs to stay up late so he can watch every game on television—always wearing his Yankees hat and baseball glove. His passion isn't surprising, really, because his dad is one of the biggest baseball aficionados I know.

As you can imagine, Danny has been chomping at the bit to play Little League baseball. Kids can join these leagues, as those of you who are parents are probably aware, as young as four or five years old. But for a variety of reasons my friend and his wife wanted Danny to be a little older before becoming part of a team. They told him that when he turned seven, they would sign him up.

A few weeks after Danny's seventh birthday, the big day arrived. On the car ride over to the sign-up location, Danny kept telling my friend that he wanted to play shortstop, like Jeter. His dad tried to explain that when you sign up for a Little League team, you don't sign up for a specific position; you just join the team. You play different positions, learn the basics, and get a taste of what baseball is all about. He told Danny that the coaches would eventually direct him toward a specific position based on his natural abilities and talents.

Of course, this concept makes perfect sense to us when it comes to Little League baseball teams. It would be crazy to sign a seven-year-old up to be a shortstop, another to play first base, and another as an outfielder without first introducing them to the game of baseball, getting to know their skills, seeing what they enjoy, and figuring out how they are gifted. Yet, when it comes to ministry, we often try to do exactly that. Why do so many of us think we need to decipher someone's gifts and get him plugged into his perfect place of service right away, without first letting him play the field? If we don't give our volunteers the chance to experiment with various areas of ministry, how can we pinpoint their gifts with any certainty? By relying on a test? It's not that simple. In *The Purpose Driven Church*, Rick Warren writes, "Most churches say, 'discover your spiritual gift and then you'll know what ministry you are supposed to have.' This is backwards. I believe the exact opposite: Start experimenting with different ministries and *then* you'll discover your gifts! Until you actually get involved in serving, you are not going to know what you're good at."[7] The logic contained within this position is exactly what Tim was explaining to David at their breakfast meeting: Part 1 of the ministry system is simply to get people involved in serving—that is, to create first-serve opportunities and encourage them into the lake, as we've discussed. Part 2 is to move them onto and up the right ministry ladder.

Cultivating the Ministry Ladder

The ministry ladder is a device to help you organize your thinking about the various volunteers, volunteer positions, and levels of volunteer engagement in your church. It functions as an accountability tool, a discipleship tool, and a measurement tool. Think through every existing ministry in your church and imagine it in terms of its own ladder. You may have a children's ministry ladder, a Sunday service ladder, a small groups ladder, a worship arts ladder, a parking team ladder, and a ladder for any other volunteer area available in your church.

When someone begins volunteering, help him identify and climb the right ministry ladder and become a regular, growing, Christlike volunteer.

When someone begins volunteering—no matter what ministry area or capacity he initially serves in—my next step and yours is to help him identify and climb the right ministry ladder and become a regular, growing, Christlike volunteer. The best way to understand how a ministry ladder works is to study a ladder in action. Let's take a look at a healthy small groups ministry ladder, since that's an area of ministry and a structure we can all probably relate to.

The Ministry Ladder in Action

Congratulations! One of your attenders who has served a few times at the Sunday service wants to become a volunteer in your groups system. Let's call her Cindy. Based on her innate abilities, her experience in various capacities at the weekend service, and her love for the small group mission, Cindy feels like groups is the area where she should take her volunteering to the next level. As such, she has volunteered to be the person who writes down and emails out her group's prayer requests each week. In our culture we call this person a group coordinator. You may think of her as an assistant leader. Her primary job is to support the group leader by being in charge of administrative tasks, and she will usually lead the group one time over the course of a semester.

By deciding to be a group coordinator, Cindy is officially on and climbing the small groups ministry ladder. Note the different rungs of the ladder in the illustration below:

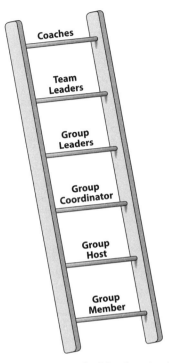

The power of the ministry ladder lies in the fact that specific qualifications and requirements come into play at each consecutive rung. Obviously someone has to be a member in a small group in order to start the trek up the small groups ministry ladder, so we'll identify group membership as the first rung. As you'll remember from the membership covenant (see chapter 5), group members are held to certain attendance, participation, and giving standards.

The next rung on the group ladder is host. Often, whoever is leading the group will host it in her own home, so this rung isn't always in play. From time to time, however, we'll come across someone who wants to serve by opening her home as a host, but who isn't ready to coordinate or lead a group.

Anyone who is a group member (and has therefore signed a group member covenant) can take the step to host, as long as they have a relatively clean and inviting home that they are willing to open up once a week over the course of a semester. We don't require our hosts to be members of the church or even that they be Christians.

The group coordinator rung—Cindy's new position—is still an entry-level position, but it carries a stronger qualification than being a host does; to serve as a coordinator, you have to be a Christian. We won't let someone who hasn't taken the step of salvation coordinate a group. So, when someone like Cindy expresses an interest in being a group coordinator, you need to have a talk with her about her salvation. Simply ask her how she came to know Christ and let her tell you her story. If she is a follower of Jesus, she can step up to the coordinator rung. If not, you may have an opportunity to lead her down the path of salvation as a result of the conversation. Otherwise, she will need to continue on simply as a group member or as a host. As a group coordinator, Cindy is still held to the requirements of the group member covenant.

The next rung on the ladder is group leader. Cindy is doing a great job as a coordinator. So great, in fact, that after a couple of semesters, her group leader suggests that she lead a group of her own. She's ready to step up to the next level. Of course, the next rung on the ladder means new requirements and new accountability. To be a group leader, Cindy must become a member of the church, if she's not already. To be candid, in our structure, we will let someone who is not a member lead for one semester, but to continue leading for a second semester, she must go through membership class and sign the membership covenant. In addition, group leaders sign and are held accountable to a Growth Group leader covenant, which encompasses and expounds upon the requirements of the group member covenant:

THE JOURNEY
Growth Group Leader Covenant

Thank you for serving as a Growth Group leader at The Journey. As a Growth Group leader you will be viewed by those in your group as a leader in the church. As a result, we ask that you enter into covenant with the other Growth Group leaders by making the following commitments:

1. I will embody and reflect the values and principles of The Journey and will follow the leadership of the staff team.
2. I will faithfully attend The Journey on Sundays and:
   - Intentionally identify and greet those in my Growth Group.
   - Participate in the church through my financial giving.
   - Lead my group in serving together once a month.
3. I will make my Growth Group a priority by:
   - Faithfully attending my Growth Group.
   - Preparing beforehand for my group each week.
   - Inviting/welcoming others to join my group.
4. I understand that I am responsible for the care of my Growth Group. As a result, I will: .
   - Pray for the individuals in my group.
   - Follow up with each person in my group.
   - Lead my group in providing care for one another.
5. I will strive to create an environment of growth in my group by:
   - Involving as many people as possible in group discussion.
   - Creating a safe, comfortable, and welcoming environment.
   - Beginning and ending on time.

_____   _____
Name   Date

Well, Cindy continues to excel. After a year or two of leading a group (only two out of the three semesters each year, of course), she is doing such a phenomenal job that you start thinking to yourself, "Wow, Cindy really has the makings of a team leader." Team leadership is the next rung on this ministry's ladder, and it is the highest volunteer position in our church. A team leader is someone who oversees and supports five group leaders.

Now, Cindy certainly can't move into such a high-capacity volunteer position unless she is fully committed to the church and to her own growth. To that end, there is a new qualification on the team leader rung: Cindy must make a commitment to tithe. (For a detailed examination of the importance of discipling our people in the biblical discipline of giving, see *Maximize: How to Develop Extravagant Givers in Your Church* [Baker, 2010].)

As you begin considering Cindy for team leadership, pull her giving records to see how well she gives. Since you don't know how much money Cindy makes, you won't know for sure if her giving reflects a full 10 percent of her income. If you are comfortable that the number you see could easily be a tithe, you may not need to have a conversation with her about her giving at all. If the number seems low, based on average incomes in your area, simply ask Cindy whether or not she is faithfully tithing her full income. All you can do is assume that she is going to answer you honestly.

If she is interested in being a team leader and is a tither—or agrees to become a tither—ask Cindy to sign the team leader covenant and then move her up the ladder. The team leader covenant looks like this:

THE JOURNEY
Growth Group Team Leader Covenant

Thank you for serving as a Growth Group team leader at The Journey. For a team leader there are expectations and responsibilities that go beyond those of a Growth Group leader. As such, you will be viewed as one of the key leaders of The Journey's Growth Groups.

As a Growth Group team leader, you are asked to enter into covenant with the other team leaders to make this ministry area a priority. To be a team leader, you are asked to make the following commitments:

1. I will embody and reflect the values of The Journey and will follow the leadership of the staff team. This includes:
   - Striving to live a godly life.
   - Attending Sunday services regularly.
   - Honoring God with my finances by tithing.
2. I understand that I am responsible for the care of the Growth Group leaders who are assigned to me. As a result, I will:
   - Pray for each of them daily.
   - Personally contact each of them weekly.
   - Meet with my team together once a semester (GG Huddle).
3. I will make attending monthly team leader meetings a priority.
4. Each semester I will assist my Growth Group coach in recruiting new Growth Group leaders and in setting up new Growth Groups.
5. I will assist with Growth Group preparation, promotion, and programs when possible (for example, GG Leaders Training, Growth Group Table, etc.).

_____   _____
Name   Date

(For a free, downloadable version of these covenants, visit www.ChurchLeaderInsights.com/connect.)

As you can see, every time Cindy steps up to a new rung on the ladder, she becomes more connected to the church and more like Jesus Christ. You want to make it easy for someone like Cindy to get on the ministry ladder that's best for her, but harder to stay at each progressive rung. As people move into higher levels of service within your church, make sure

Make it easy to get on the ladder, but harder to stay at each progressive rung.

they are being carefully discipled and are becoming more fully developing followers of Jesus at every step along the way.

Here's what the small groups ministry ladder looks like with the corresponding qualifications attached to each rung:

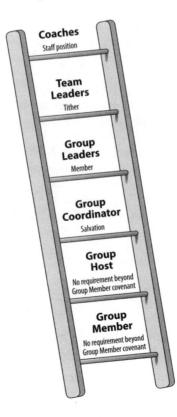

Coaches
Staff position

Team Leaders
Tither

Group Leaders
Member

Group Coordinator
Salvation

Group Host
No requirement beyond Group Member covenant

Group Member
No requirement beyond Group Member covenant

Using this ladder as a guide, take every ministry area in your church and define its unique ladder. How many rungs does each ladder have? What expectations correlate with what rungs? How far up the ladder can a volunteer climb without being a follower of Jesus, a church member, a tither, or whatever other checkpoint you consider important? Without a structure like the ministry ladder in place, you run the all-too-common risk of moving immature Christians into high levels of leadership before they are ready. Eventually this creates a breakdown. You end up with a worship leader who isn't tithing or a head greeter who has never taken the step of membership. The resulting problems can be enormous, as we'll examine in chapter 7.

Structuring the Ministry Ladder

Have you ever had to climb up a weak, rickety ladder to change a lightbulb or paint the side of a house? Remember that feeling? I bet you took every step cautiously, not quite sure if the ladder was going to support you. Compare that to the secure feeling of climbing a big steel ladder—one that is structurally sound and built well for its job. All ladders are not created equal. Their constitution determines their quality. Similarly, your ministry ladder can be either rickety or strong, depending on the work you put into its construction. As you begin thinking about every ministry in your church in terms of the ministry ladder, make sure you define the structure for success by taking these four steps:

1. *Structure for Growth, Not Control.* Don't fall into the trap of structuring for control; instead think in terms

113

of what will help you connect the maximum number of volunteers. One of the best ways to structure for growth rather than control is to steer away from putting mature commitments too low on the ladder. For example, don't put church membership too low. Have some rungs below salvation. Let your volunteers step up a rung or two before requiring that they do anything. Give people a chance to get committed to the ladder. As they become more committed to their area of service, they'll become more committed to following Jesus's best plan for their lives; they will be ready for the more mature commitments you'll be asking them to make. If you put those commitments too low in an attempt at control, you will lose a huge number of climbers.

2. *Structure for Stress and Release.* Let your structure breathe by giving people permission to take time off. You may want to refer back to the discussion of the principle of stress and release in chapter 3. Building the truth of this principle into your ministry ladder will make every area of service run more smoothly. One of the reasons we have so few problems with our ministry leaders is that, just as a problem becomes a problem, it's usually time for that person to step away for a rest period. The release time gives us an opportunity to address any issues and make any necessary corrections in that volunteer's alignment with the church and with the specifics of his service position.

Not to mention, a break gives your dedicated volunteers a chance to serve in other areas of the church, allowing them to remain connected to the big picture.

For example, when someone who is consistently on the worship team moves into a release period, she may want to serve as an usher or a greeter for a few Sundays. She'll stay connected through service, see the church from a different perspective, and meet some new people, all while taking a needed break from her standard serving position.

3. *Structure for Measurability.* Build in measurement points at every level of your ministry ladder. Any time you can, attach an expectation or a covenant to a specific rung and then hold people accountable. That way you can use your ladder to measure growth and involvement.

One of the most vital steps you can take is to make sure you capture people's information as early as possible. When someone steps onto the lowest rung of a ladder, do you know who she is and how to contact her so you can invite her to serve again? One of the worst mistakes we ever made early on was letting people serve in entry-level ministry positions and failing to get their full names and contact information. We had people interested enough in serving to step onto a ladder, but we didn't know who they were or how to follow up with them.

When you have your volunteers' information, you can invite them to take a specific next step and continue their progression into deeper service and maturity. Having this information is also what allows you to measure your overall system effectively. You'll know exactly how many people you have on each rung and how long they've been there. (For more details on what to measure and how, download my free resource *What Gets Measured*, at www.ChurchLeaderInsights.com/connect.)

4. *Structure for Care.* You need to have a structure in place to care for your volunteers. Often when we think of providing care, we think of visiting someone in the hospital or preparing a meal for a family if a loved one passes away. But care runs much deeper. How well do you know your volunteers? What's going on in their lives? When are their birthdays and their anniversaries? Do you celebrate milestone moments like marriage with them? We'll dig into this more in the next section.

Climbing the Right Ladder

In Romans 12:6 Paul writes to the Roman church, "In his grace, God has given us different gifts for doing certain things well." Paul's assertion is echoed many times over throughout the Scriptures. God has molded us and made us for a particular purpose (Ps. 139:13–16). A manifestation of the Holy Spirit is given to each and every one of us so that we can use it to do our part in building the church (1 Cor. 12:7). We have been uniquely crafted and formed into the individuals we are by a God who loves us—and who allows us to know ourselves pretty well.

As a friend of mine likes to say, just look to the animals for a lesson in gifting. God created every animal with unique qualities for a unique purpose. Some animals run and hunt; some animals burrow and nest; some are social while others are loners. The animals didn't choose their nature—God did.

And together they comprise a wonderful, diverse, fully functioning animal kingdom. To my knowledge, no animal has ever taken a gifts assessment test or gone through extensive directed training to know its role. Kangaroos just started hopping. Gazelles just started running. They innately knew what they were created for.

As human beings created in God's image, we are more complex than our animal counterparts. Still, we can learn something from their willingness to acknowledge and dive right into their God-given roles. Finding the right fit for our people within the kaleidoscope of our church's ministry is often not nearly as difficult as we would have it be. In my experience, most people know deep down how they are gifted and what area of ministry they are best suited for without much guidance at all.

Nine times out of ten, if you allow a new server the leeway to volunteer in several different areas and find his way toward the ladder that he feels most drawn to, he will choose the ladder that God created him to climb. The spiritual gifts test he takes later will likely reflect what he already knew. While such assessments have their place, they generally just confirm what people already understand to be their God-given nature and direction. I don't want to oversimplify this, but at the same time I want to warn you against overcomplicating it. You and I definitely have a responsibility to help people uncover their unique talents and guide them in the right direction; let's not make it more difficult than it actually is.

At The Journey, we teach on serving at least three times every year and do a serving series once every three years, as I've recommended you do. As part of that teaching, we discuss the biblical imperative of discovering one's unique gifting and encourage people to use the *SHAPE* spiritual assessment tool to help them definitively pinpoint the right path for their service. *SHAPE* is an acronym for the five elements that determine what someone's ministry should be—Spiritual gifts, Heart, Abilities, Personality, and Experiences. (For more on SHAPE, see *SHAPE: Finding and Fulfilling Your Unique Purpose for Life* by Erik Rees [Zondervan, 2006]. For free downloads of messages I've done to mobilize people to serve, visit www.ChurchLeaderInsights.com/connect.)

Other spiritual assessment tests and methods are available, and volumes have been written on identifying spiritual gifts, so I won't go into detail here. I do, however, implore you to use such assessments and tests as a tool, not as a be-all and end-all determining factor. Trust that your people know how God has created them.

When your new volunteers step onto the right ministry ladder and start to move up, you will see healthy growth begin to happen in their lives, in each respective ministry and in your church as a whole. May we never shrink from doing what's necessary to build people and build the church for God's glory.

7

lessons learned
the hard way

SUGGESTIONS, TIPS, AND TACTICS

Abandon all hopes of utopia—there are people involved.

—Clayton Cramer

If you need wisdom, ask our generous God, and he will give it to you. He will not rebuke you for asking. But when you ask him, be sure that your faith is in God alone. Do not waver, for a person with divided loyalty is as unsettled as a wave of the sea that is blown and tossed by the wind.

—James 1:5–6

You never escape time in the trenches without a few battle wounds. Developing the ministry system as it is detailed here could definitely be considered trench time, and my team and I have the scars to prove it—which is great news for you! As you move forward in implementing this system in your church, I want you to benefit from the hard-learned lessons that have propelled our ministry system to its current level of effectiveness in our church and in thousands of others around the world. Here are some suggestions, tips, and tactics to live by as you work toward doubling your volunteer base.

Suggestions (Read: Warnings)

Clearly define the complete ladder of a ministry before you let anyone climb on. No one wants to climb a rickety ladder—and believe me, you don't want that, either. It's way too dangerous. Before a single new volunteer steps on, think through what each level of your ministry ladder looks like in detail. Define the progression of the rungs. If you don't know enough about a certain ministry area to thoroughly outline the levels, invite your key people who are already volunteering in that area into the discussion. They'll be able to provide more insight than you may realize—and they'll appreciate the opportunity to have input into an area that's important to them.

Have some positions on the ladder that non-Christians can fill. Remember the Florida church from chapter 4—the one that decided to let non-Christians serve in the parking lot? Those unbelieving guys were able to step up to the first rung of the parking lot ministry ladder even though they weren't Christians. As a result, they had the chance to get to know and learn from some mature believers higher up on the ladder. Those more mature guys were key in modeling Christianity to the non-Christians and guiding them down the path of salvation. If the unbelievers hadn't had the option of getting on the ladder until after they put their faith in Jesus, well, they may never have become Christians.

Remember, believing does not have to precede belonging in the process of becoming. Don't let tradition or unexamined thinking be a stumbling block in someone's journey toward salvation. What harm can come from letting an unbeliever direct cars into parking spaces, hand out programs, or man the refreshment table? None—but the rewards of allowing someone to belong can be enormous.

Create a position description that defines each rung of the ladder and have volunteers sign it. In the parlance of small groups, these position descriptions are the covenants that our volunteers sign along the way. The first covenant is simply the group member covenant, on the lowest rungs of the ladder. Then there's the group leader covenant and the team leader covenant, as we discussed in chapter 6. On other ministry ladders where you may not have actual covenants to put in place, you need to create a clear position description for each rung of the ladder, review that position description when a new volunteer steps up, and have him sign it.

Clarity is key. Expectations must be clearly defined and agreed upon. For example, in your children's ministry, decide what regulations and expectations need to be in place at each rung of the ladder. Maybe as part of the entry-level position descriptions, every volunteer agrees to never be in a room alone with a child and to wash her hands before serving. As a volunteer moves up the ladder in children's ministry, perhaps there is a CPR requirement. Maybe part of a certain rung's responsibility is to make sure that setup is done by a specific time or that parents get checked in a specific way. You will need to decide what responsibilities and expectations come at what rungs. Those decisions will be unique to your church.

Agreements prevent disagreements.

Agreements prevent disagreements. Present each volunteer with a detailed description of his responsibilities before he steps onto any rung of the ladder. Have him sign the position description as an acknowledgment that he understands what is expected of him. Keep a file of these signed covenants or position descriptions, and hold your people accountable to them; you will circumvent countless problems and save yourself a lot of frustration and stress down the line. Trust me.

Hold people accountable for their level. When you make agreements on the front end of a relationship, you are free to hold people accountable to those agreements. In fact, if you don't hold them accountable, you are doing them a disservice. For instance, if you ask someone to begin honoring God financially as part of the requirement for a certain rung, the impetus is on you to check her giving. If she stops giving, she relinquishes her right to serve. You can't assume that because she signed the position description saying she would give that she will remain consistent. You have to stay on top of things. You don't get what you expect; you get what you inspect. If her giving stalls, it's probably a warning sign that something else is wrong. You owe it to her to follow up and make sure everything is okay.

Similarly, don't assume that because someone is at a certain level one semester—say a team leader on the groups ladder—that she gets stay at that level the next semester. Check her records. Is she attending? Is she involved? Is she giving? Is she growing? At every rung of every ministry ladder, make sure your people are doing what is expected of them. Staying in touch with your volunteers' commitments is not just important for your ministry system; it's important for monitoring the state of each individual's spiritual walk.

> *You don't get what you expect; you get what you inspect.*

Beware of the person who wants to climb the rungs of the ladder but doesn't want to fulfill the requirements. One of the darkest moments in our church came as a result of not heeding this warning. Many years ago, a gregarious, charismatic guy we'll call Steve (not his real name) was on one of the ministry ladders, progressing rapidly up the rungs. He had actually made it to a high level on the ladder without adhering to the expectations along the way, which was our fault. Once Steve had stepped into this relatively significant position of leadership, I started getting a bad vibe from him. He would avoid me after the service; he seemed distant with other leaders; I overheard him talking to people on his team in a questionable way a few times. I quickly began to get uncomfortable.

My first step in response to these signs of trouble was to look into Steve's records. I found an immediate red flag—Steve had never gone through membership class. Next, I pulled his giving record and found that he actually gave well. (As an aside, whenever I have a question about someone, one of the first things I do is pull his giving. A person's giving can tell you a lot about how connected his heart is to the church and how mature he is.) I was happy to see Steve's strong giving, but that didn't negate the fact that he had never become a member. So we sat him down and had a conversation with him about the importance of membership class. He made the excuse that he had a commitment to another church and wanted to keep that previous commitment for the time being. He said that if we would give him a little space, he would become a member. So we let him stay in his position based on that promise. Bad decision.

A few months later, flying under the radar, Steve moved up to the next rung on the ladder. He directly influenced dozens of other volunteers and had access to a whole database of people in our church. Again too late, we asked ourselves, "Wait, did Steve ever go through membership class?" He hadn't. (We weren't too quick on the uptake back then.) I bet you can guess where this story is going. Within three months of becoming a team leader, Steve left the church and took a number of people with him—people from all different rungs of the ministry ladder. We lost members, committed regular attenders, and people who hadn't even taken the step of salvation yet.

Steve was able to advance to a level that allowed him to cause significant destruction because we failed to hold him accountable to the basic requirements of the ministry ladder. Consequently he wasn't on board with the vision or mission for the church, nor was he committed to the requirements of being a member or a team leader. He progressed through the levels of leadership without agreeing to the accompanying expectations, and disaster followed. We can't blame Steve; the responsibility was on our shoulders to hold him accountable, and we didn't. You may have a similar story in your church. Unfortunately, situations like this are all too common thanks to our collective failure to establish guidelines and hold people accountable. The ministry ladder gives you an effective tool for tracking the growth and commitment of your people as they move through the volunteering ranks. I contend that when you get the accountability aspect of the ladder right, everything else in your ministry system will fall into place.

Tips and Tactics

Allow people to switch ladders. Part of helping people discover how God has wired them is letting them try the lower rungs of several different ladders before committing to one. When you give new volunteers the freedom to get to know the entry-level rungs of a few different ladders, they will be better able to identify the one they feel most called to. Build this give-and-take into your system; let them know that trying different areas is okay. Early on in their service, volunteers shouldn't be looked down upon for jumping around. The problem comes when they serve on too many ladders for too long or climb to the higher rungs of more than one ladder.

Tim and David both pull out their wallets and plunk down enough money to cover the bill and their waiter's tip. Tim can tell that David still isn't quite ready to leave. Now that he has seen a glimmer of hope for expanding his one-man show, he's eager to get all of his questions answered.

"Hey David, if I send a quick email, I can push my next meeting forward thirty minutes or so. . . . How about you? I feel like there's more we need to talk about," Tim says.

"I was actually just thinking the same thing. Yep, let's do it."

Both men grab their phones, bang out an email, and then settle back in. Tim signals the waiter for one more round of coffee.

"So, you were saying something about keeping the ladders fluid early on . . ." David prompts Tim back to the conversation at hand.

"Right, you want your new volunteers to be able to serve wherever they want for a while before they make a decision on what ladder to climb, so let them jump between the lower rungs of several ladders. Don't get frustrated with them for doing that—and tell your volunteer leaders not to get frustrated. People have to try things out before they can find their place."

"Sure. If they don't explore the options, they may not be able to tap into what kind of service makes them come alive," David says. "I get that."

"Right. But be careful at the same time—don't let them start climbing too high on the rungs of more than one ladder, because that can lead to trouble. Let me tell you a quick story about a woman in my church named Liz. Liz and her husband, Jon, first showed up at church because a co-worker of Jon's invited them. They became Christians; they became members; they started tithing; they got their kids plugged into our children's area. Pretty quickly, I watched them blossom into strong members of the community. They are a great couple."

"Seems like you have mentioned them before . . ." David says.

"Probably. Anyway, about ten months ago, Liz started volunteering in entry-level positions on a couple of different ladders. She wanted to try out the worship arts ladder and the small groups ladder. So she started singing on the worship team and coordinating a women's small group. She was great in both areas, which actually created a problem."

"What kind of problem?"

"Well, the leaders on both the worship arts ladder and on the small groups ladder loved her. They both kept inviting her to climb up to the next rung. So she did. After about six months of serving at a higher level on both ladders, Liz was completely burned out."

"Oh, gotcha," David says. "Wow, that would burn anybody out."

"When I saw the warning signs, I asked Liz to come to my office. I wanted to have a conversation with her about what was going on. She told me that she loved both areas of ministry, but that she just couldn't keep up her current volunteering pace. Still, she was afraid of letting other leaders down if she stepped away from either ladder. I made sure she understood that she wouldn't be letting anyone down by picking one ministry to commit to, but when I asked her which ladder she wanted to stay with, she honestly didn't know. She loved and excelled on both."

"That's a gifted volunteer," David says.

"She is. So, I encouraged her to take a couple of months off to rest, get some perspective, and pray about the area of service she should continue with. She did. When she came back rested and clear, she chose small groups. Now she is one of our best team leaders on that ladder."

"So, letting people try out different ladders on the lower rungs is important. Just don't let them climb up the rungs on more than one," David summarizes, as he makes a couple of notes.

"You got it."

People need some time to find their place. In my experience the ladder someone begins on is not usually the ladder he stays on. Often I will hear a volunteer say something like, "I really wanted to get involved in groups, but then I found my place of service over in children's ministry." Now, he may still be a small group host or even a coordinator and also climb to a high rung on the children's ministry ladder. Staying on a low rung of a second ladder is okay if he is gung ho and can handle it. The trouble shows up when volunteers, like Liz, climb too high on more than one ladder. As you give people the freedom to find their place, make sure your overachievers don't get themselves into a situation that could lead to burnout.

Use timelines to encourage people to take a break from serving. One of the most common questions I come across in regard to dealing with volunteers is, "How do I fire a problem volunteer?" When you put timelines on service, as we've already discussed in detail, you never have to fire a volunteer; you simply let his term expire and then you don't invite him to serve again. More often than not, a break solves any problems you may be having.

With time and experience, you will figure out exactly how long it takes from the moment someone steps onto a specific rung of the ladder to determine if that step was right for him. For example, in our small groups structure, we know that it only takes one semester—two at the most—to determine if someone is on the right rung of the ladder. On the worship arts ladder, it usually takes about six months to verify whether or not someone has stepped up to the right position. In children's ministry, we can tell within a month. Other areas may require longer timelines. For instance, once someone new has committed to serving as an usher, it may take a year to see whether or not he is in the right position. Once you get a feel for these various timeframes, use them to guide the timelines you put on each area of service.

Always challenge people to go to the next level. As volunteers move higher on the ministry ladder, they will grow in maturity. Part of discipling your people, then, is to continually challenge them to take the next step on the ladder they are climbing.

There is a caveat to this rule. At some point each one of your volunteers is going to hit his sweet spot. He will find that rung on the ladder where he engages effectively and won't necessarily need to climb any higher. For instance, a lot of volunteers on the small groups ladder advance to the group leader rung and stay there. That's okay. At that rung they are

---

Church Leader Testimony

The ministry system significantly impacted ministry in our church. Before implementing these principles, we struggled with the same small number of people doing everything and getting burned out—and we had the mentality of constantly *needing* volunteers. The seminar changed our perspective: we don't have *needs*; we have *opportunities* for people to use their God-given resources to participate in advancing God's kingdom.

Thanks to this system, we also refined our process for plugging people in. We became more organized in utilizing teams on a rotation for a specific time frame. We intentionally built in empty positions to create opportunities to plug in new servers. The ministry ladder concept helped us identify our expectations and requirements for our people at different levels of service and leadership in each area of the ministry. Now, over 50 percent of our regular attendance is actively serving in ministry in any given week.

Pastor Michael McAvoy
Open Arms Community Church, Bradford, Pennsylvania

---

being held to a high level of accountability and have grown to a significant point of maturity. Not everyone will be gifted or called to move up to the team leader rung. A similar level exists on each of your ministry ladders. Once a volunteer reaches that level, it's fine to allow him to remain static. The key is to define that rung on each ladder.

When volunteers are on the lower rungs, however, you should be continually encouraging them up the rungs into deeper service and growth. If someone is on a lower rung of a ladder and doesn't want to move up or doesn't feel like she can, she needs to find a different ladder where she will be able to become more of a servant. If she's not willing to find a place where she can truly connect, she may just be keeping you at arm's length, which gives you a different problem to address altogether.

Consider compensating High Capacity Volunteers. At a certain point, a volunteer becomes so important to his ministry area that he qualifies as a High Capacity Volunteer (HCV). High Capacity Volunteers have reached a level that surpasses the highest expectations of regular volunteers, but aren't quite on par with your paid staff. This upside-down pyramid illustrates how the ministry system can actually serve as a funnel to staffing, and where HCVs fit into that flow:

When a volunteer reaches the HCV level, whether you see future staff potential or not, you may want to consider compensating him for his time and energy. As such, I also refer to HCVs as $50-a-week volunteers. Let me give you an example.

Imagine that you have a group of three or four people who run your soundboard, with one High Capacity Volunteer who is in charge. The HCV may have great leadership abilities and be a little more technically savvy than the rest of the team.

He's also extremely dependable; you know he is going to be there to make sure you have sound on Sunday, even if no one else shows up. Over time, you may end up having an A, B, and C sound team, and this one volunteer is the clear choice to be in charge of all three. He has become so important to you that you need him to serve every week. The thought of losing him scares you. At this point you should approach Mr. Soundboard and invite him to be a $50-a-week volunteer. Say something along the lines of:

> What you are doing is extremely valuable. I know you are probably not going to want me to do this, but I want to reward you in some way for being here so faithfully and doing what you do. I'd like to provide you with some basic compensation, maybe just to help with your gas expense or with some of the meals you eat on the road as a result of your service. Let's clarify your exact responsibilities, so we are both agreed on them, and then I'd like to start giving you $50 per week.

Essentially you are buying a deeper level of clarity and commitment without bringing him on as part-time staff. Most important, making someone like this soundboard whiz a $50-a-week volunteer assures you tremendous accountability. (For more on how we use this staffing process at The Journey, see my staffing resources at www.ChurchLeader Insights.com/connect.)

When we first started The Journey, our initial four or five "employees" were $50-a-week HCVs. They weren't true part-time employees because I couldn't afford to pay them a part-time salary. But the $50-a-week reward made them extremely accountable and dedicated. More recently, this is how I often start someone out who has future staff potential. They become a $50-a-week volunteer and then make the jump to either administrative staff or part-time staff.

Celebrate and reward each step taken. Take the time to celebrate and reward your volunteers as they climb the rungs of the ministry ladder. Don't be afraid to ask people how they want to be rewarded when they have done a great job or achieved a major accomplishment. Know what motivates them. We'll discuss this in detail in part 4. For now, just remember that reward and celebration are key components of encouraging your volunteers and keeping them excited about serving.

Ask people how they want to be rewarded.

The ministry ladder structure gives you the opportunity to continually invite your people into deeper fellowship with Jesus through increased servanthood. As you call volunteers to climb the ladder, you are offering them the chance to use the talents, gifts, and abilities God gave them in a way that will have eternal significance. You may be leading them into becoming more than a volunteer; you may be helping them toward a life of ministry at a higher level than they ever imagined.

8

calling out the called

GUIDING PEOPLE INTO FULL-TIME
VOCATIONAL MINISTRY

The call to ministry is the call to prepare.

—Anonymous

Now these are the gifts Christ gave to the church: the apostles,
the prophets, the evangelists, and the pastors and teachers.

—Ephesians 4:11

No discussion of connecting people to ministry would be
complete without addressing the highest level of ministry
involvement—the call to full-time vocational ministry. If you
are a pastor or an ordained staff member, as most of you
reading this likely are, you probably have some understanding

of what I mean by the "call to ministry." Still, since it's used in such a variety of ways in various circles, the term can get confusing. If you've ever had a vacancy on your church staff, perhaps you have *extended a call* to someone to fill that role. If you were in need of another pastor, you probably *extended a call* to someone who had been *called* into full-time pastoral ministry. We also talk frequently about people *being called* to different positions within the church, which doesn't necessarily mean they are *called* to ministry as a career. That is, unless they have *received a call* for a position, such as the pinnacle of all *callings*—the call to preach. Confused yet?

Needless to say, the issue of calling raises a lot of questions. Do you have to be called to be an active volunteer or to be on a church staff? What exactly is this elusive "call to ministry," and to whom does it apply? And given our current discussion, how does it fit into the ministry system? Let's take a deeper look at the issue of calling and try to clarify some of these questions.

The Call to Ministry

There are two primary ways that those of us who understand church-speak intend for the term "calling" to be interpreted. First of all, as professional church leaders, we like to use the word "call" in lieu of the word "hire." When we want to invite someone into a staff position, we extend a call to that person (as mentioned above), which basically means we are making him an offer. I can't tell you exactly why we phrase the proposition this way; I suppose it sounds more spiritual to say "extend a call" than to say "make an offer."

The second and most common way people in the church use the term "call" is in reference to someone being "called to ministry"—which is what the rest of this chapter will focus on. Wrapping our minds around the call to ministry is particularly important to our examination of the ministry system. Before we dive in, however, let me say that this chapter is not meant to be a theological treatise on the call to ministry nor will it examine the various roles of ministry that people can be called to. (For a list of in-depth resources on this topic, visit www.ChurchLeaderInsights.com/connect.)

Discerning the Call

The call to ministry strikes all of us in unique ways and at supremely individualized times. I first sensed the call to ministry during my freshman year of college. One of my best friends, also a pastor, knew that he was called to ministry just before his freshman year of high school. I recently met someone at one of my training events who was called after a long and successful career with a power company. In each of these instances, the term "call" refers specifically to an innate desire to go into full-time ministry. When it comes to prompting us toward professional service in his kingdom, God has a different path for each of us. Even so, the essence of this calling is the same.

God initiates his plan for a person's vocational commitment through the ongoing and often extremely persistent prompting of the Holy Spirit in that person's life. When someone feels the prompting of the Spirit, he has an obligation to enter into careful prayer, to spend ample time studying God's Word in relation to the prompting, and to seek out the affirmation of strong spiritual counsel. These three channels help the person who feels prompted to discern whether or not the prompting is valid. The decision to go into full-time ministry can't be arrived at lightly; it is a serious call. Professional ministry is more than just a commitment to a career path—it is the complete surrender of all other vocational options for the sole focus of serving in ministry on the mission field, in the local church, or in supporting agencies.

There are many ministry roles that a person may feel called to. Part of the discerning process is figuring out what role God intends the person he is prompting to step into. Most commonly, however, people who are called into ministry are called to be pastors—and what a calling that is. As you and I are well aware, the role of a pastor is to serve as the primary equipper, shepherd, and leader of a local body of believers who have accepted and affirmed the pastor's leadership in that church. Then, with the understanding that Christ is the head of the church, the pastor seeks to wisely lead and direct the church along the proper path. Again, it's a serious call—and not always easy to discern or accept. Maybe a look at my own story can shed some additional light here.

Understanding My Call

Before God changed my direction, I was on the fast track to becoming an engineer—which probably explains my penchant for logic and systems throughout my books and resources. In 1990, while pursuing my degree in electrical engineering, I began to sense that God was calling me to a different path. Now this sense wasn't an excuse to shirk hard classes; I wasn't flunking engineering. In fact, I was doing quite well academically. It wasn't that I knew a lot of passionate, charismatic pastors who drew me in either; I only knew two pastors at the time. And it wasn't that I wanted a career in local church ministry. If you had held a gun to my head, I wouldn't have been able to articulate what a career in ministry would look like.

So how did I know God was calling me? Every time I read Scripture, prayed, listened to a sermon, or spent time with Christian friends, I sensed an internal prompting to change paths and enter full-time church work. After several weeks of being unable to shake this sense of nudging, I tracked down my pastor at the time and told him what was going on. I was expecting a big pat on the back and a welcome-to-ministry hug, so I was pretty surprised when he tried to talk me out of it. Later I learned that he was just following the example of great pastors of the past who have dealt with young people and their sense of calling. The only way he could know for sure that I was called, he told me, was to be convinced that I couldn't be talked out of it.

Lecturing his students on the details of ministry over a century ago, Charles Spurgeon said:

> The first sign of the heavenly call is an intense, all-absorbing desire for the work. In order to be a true call to the ministry there must be an irresistible, overwhelming craving and raging thirst for telling to others what God has done to our own souls. . . . "Do not enter the ministry if you can help it," was the deeply sage advice of a divine to one who sought his judgment. If any student in this room could be content to be a newspaper editor, or a grocer, or a farmer, or a doctor, or a lawyer, or a senator, or a king, in the name of heaven

and earth let him go his way; he is not the man in whom dwells the Spirit of God in its fullness, for a man so filled with God would utterly weary of any pursuit but that for which his inmost soul pants. If on the other hand, you can say that for all the wealth of both the Indies you could not and dare not espouse any other calling so as to be put aside from preaching the gospel of Jesus Christ, then, depend upon it, if other things be equally satisfactory, you have the signs of this apostleship.[8]

> *"'Do not enter the ministry if you can help it,' was the deeply sage advice of a divine to one who sought his judgment."*
> —Charles Spurgeon

After a period of counseling with my now-convinced pastor, as well as some biblical and practical exploration on my part, I decided to leave the engineering path and pursue a career in ministry. A few months later, I enrolled in a bachelor of religion program at a great undergraduate school. The rest is history. Once God started prompting me into his service, I understood that everything needed to change. I simply knew that ministry in general—and pastoring in particular—was my career path. I am called to ministry. I am called because I know I am called.

Can you relate to my story? Or was your call into ministry completely different? Take a minute to reflect on your own calling. What was going on in your life when you were called? How would you articulate your calling? God is not predictable when it comes to how he prompts someone into his service. He devises a plan to usurp our path, based on our unique makeup, desires, and experiences. He calls each of us individually, yet, once called, we all know that we are called. Of course, given deeper study, you will find that there are logical and biblical requisites to determine with complete assurance that someone has been called. But at its core the best way to understand and articulate the power of my calling and likely yours is this: we are called because we know we are called.

The Challenge of the Call

What are you doing to help people in your church discern God's call to ministry? How would you help someone who may feel called move forward? I shared my calling and invited you to think about yours for one reason: we as church leaders need a fresh mindset and a new imperative when it comes to challenging the people in our churches who may be called to full-time ministry. Think about it. When was the last time you heard someone preach on the call to ministry? Or even teach a sliver of a message on the topic? When was the last time you invited people, young and old, to answer the call to ministry in your church? What are you doing this week, this month, or this year to help people discern God's potential call on their life?

We as church leaders need a fresh mindset and a new imperative when it comes to challenging the people in our churches who may be called to full-time ministry.

Our discussion throughout these pages is about connecting volunteers with God's best through serving, and moving them to the heights of his plan for them. At the supreme level, that means helping those few who are called to full-time ministry to realize and answer that call. You might want to think of the call to ministry as the highest rung on the ministry ladder—it's not a rung that people can aspire to based on their own will but rather a rung that God has to invite them to. While it may not be reached often, it's a rung we can't ignore.

As we connect people to places of service in our church, we should continually be aware that some of those people just might be the men and women God wants to call into vocational ministry. Obviously the call to full-time ministry is in no way a requirement to serve—every one of our people is called to serve on some level—so we have to be careful neither to set our focus too high nor to inadvertently place the bar out of reach. At the same time, as we see people eagerly scaling the rungs of the ministry ladder, especially young people, we must not shy away from introducing a conversation about the call to ministry and helping them articulate the prompting they may be feeling deep down.

At The Journey we have been fortunate to see over a dozen men and women called out of our congregation and into full-time ministry. These individuals are now scattered around the globe, working in various churches or parachurch organizations. While I'm thankful that God used The Journey as part of his plan for the lives of these young servants, I often wonder if the number should actually be much higher. I have to confess I haven't always done everything I could to raise awareness about the call to ministry. It's a system I'm still working on.

To speak candidly, I have to say that of all the chapters in this book this one is the most in-process one for me personally. Yes, I want to challenge 50 percent or more of our churchgoers to serve at least one hour a week in the ministry of the church, for the cause of Christ and their own spiritual development.

But I also want to be on the lookout for the one, two, or three people along the way whom God might be planning to raise up to be pastors on our staff, or who are called to lead new churches or to pastor existing churches in need.

My challenge to you—and to myself—is this: as you lead and equip your church, be diligent in connecting people to places of service; but, as you do, don't forget to cooperate with God in calling out the called for the sake of Christ. (For a list of resources on the call to ministry or to learn more if you think you are being called to ministry, visit www. ChurchLeaderInsights.com/connect.)

PART 4

celebrating
and reproducing
servants

9

ongoing recruitment and reproduction

THE KEY TO A CONSTANT FLOW OF VOLUNTEERS

People want to be part of something larger than themselves. They want to be part of something they're really proud of, that they'll fight for, sacrifice for, that they trust.

—Howard Schultz

During the forty days after his crucifixion, he appeared to the apostles from time to time, and he proved to them in many ways that he was actually alive. And he talked to them about the Kingdom of God.

—Acts 1:3

A few weeks ago, I caught the second half of an NFL football game on television. The game was close—it ended up coming down to a field goal in the last five seconds—but honestly I was having a hard time concentrating on the game itself. I couldn't stop thinking about a fan they had shown on camera at the beginning of the fourth quarter. The man was so decked out in face paint, hair paint, and body paint that you couldn't see a single cell of his real hair or skin. On top of the paint, he was wearing an outrageous mascot costume and what looked like five pounds of jewelry. He was on his feet, screaming toward the field with passion that is rarely seen in any other situation.

This fan defined fanatical. He fascinated me, not because I hadn't seen his type before—of course I had. We've all seen the team extremists who go to unbelievable lengths to identify themselves as hard-core devotees. But for some reason, on that particular night, I couldn't get away from the realization that what this crazy fan was doing was grasping at a momentary opportunity to be a part of something bigger than himself. Cleaned up and sitting across a dinner table from you, he would probably just say that he likes football, gets excited about his team, and wants to show his support. But his actions prove that his need to connect runs deeper than being a simple football enthusiast.

If you look around, you can see the pull to be involved in something bigger than ourselves play out in all kinds of areas. People go berserk over celebrities and even worship music icons. They bond over extreme politics and become oddly obsessed with their kid's soccer team. Why? Because God has created in each and every one of us a yearning to be connected to himself and actively involved in his purposes on this earth. Our spirit knows we are meant to be part of a larger enterprise than our limited daily concerns.

As Saint Augustine famously said, "Thou hast made us for thyself, O Lord, and our hearts are restless until they find their rest in thee."[9] As a result, we often end up trying to find our place of belonging, camaraderie, and passion in things like sports, entertainment, and politics. These things are bigger than we are, yes, but not nearly as big as the kingdom of God. Don't misunderstand me: there is absolutely nothing wrong with being a sports fan, following a musician, or being enthusiastic about political issues. The problem comes when we, or our people, try to use those things to compensate for the deep connection to God and his work that our heart is seeking.

Your members and attenders have a strong, innate pull to be engaged in kingdom service. As we've discussed in these pages, putting the framework in place to get them involved and then keep them involved is essential to discipling them into God's best for their lives. Serving leads to maturity; it gives them ownership in the church and deepens their walk with Jesus. Once you have created first-serve opportunities to get people involved and then helped them find, climb onto, and begin advancing up the right ministry ladder, your next goal should be to continually reproduce strong, faithful servants—that is, to continually connect people's yearning hearts to God's best plan for their lives.

A Formula for Future Volunteers

As you may have realized by now, I am mathematically minded. I think in terms of boxes and graphs and formulas. That's just the way God wired me. Thankfully, he has been able to work through that wiring to break down ethereal concepts and communicate them clearly for the growth and glory of the kingdom. So, keeping in step with my nature, I've developed a formula for reproducing volunteers. Would you expect any less?

While the formula for future volunteers may look big and hairy at first to those of you who aren't equation lovers, it's really quite simple. Trust me. Are you ready? Here's the key to having a constant flow of new volunteers at your church:

GE + TL + CTR + AM + GN = Constant Flow of New Volunteers!

If you miss any one of the steps in this formula, you are never going to have enough volunteers. But if you get all of these pieces right, you will always have a constant flow of new volunteers. Let's examine each of the variables of the formula.

Good Experience (GE). Making sure your volunteers have a good experience when they serve is key to reproducing volunteers. Positive buzz is a powerful thing. If volunteers have a good time—if they feel useful, well connected, and engaged—they are going to talk about it to their friends in the church. They are going to invite other people to serve with them. On the other hand, if they don't have a good experience, they will probably let people know that too . . . and you can forget about them getting anyone else involved.

Not to mention, your nonserving attenders and members are keenly perceptive. They will usually be able to tell whether or not the people serving at the weekend service are having a good experience just by looking at them. At The Journey, we have an overflow of people who want to get involved in children's ministry. I'm convinced that one of the reasons so many people are interested in that area is that they always see our children's volunteers having such a great time. When parents drop their kids off, the volunteers are whistling, laughing, playing, eating snacks, making crafts; they are having fun serving. When other potential servers see the joy that can come with serving, they want to get involved.

Timeline (TL). We've already discussed serving timelines at length, so I won't go into it again here. Just remember, always put a timeline on service.

Challenge to Reproduce (CTR). Constantly challenge your servers to think in terms of reproducing their ministry area. People generally rise to a challenge; it gives them a goal and motivates them to step out of their comfort zone. Simply challenging your volunteers to find and invite new volunteers to serve in their area of ministry will go a long way toward getting new people connected.

If your key volunteers understand the thinking behind your ministry system, they will be even more likely to see the importance of reproducing. For example, explain to them how timelines open up new serving opportunities for others. Explain A-B-C teams so they understand the potential for growth. If you currently only have one worship team, and you haven't taken the time to explain your ministry strategy to them, your key worship team volunteers may think, "Oh, we are pretty full; we don't really have room for anyone else on the team so I'm not going to try to recruit anyone." But if they see the potential of having multiple worship teams with strong, eager people involved, they will step up to the challenge of reproducing.

Accountability and Motivation (AM). Holding people accountable for the job they've agreed to do is essential on many levels. As we've seen, accountability comes through agreed-upon position descriptions or covenants. Motivation comes through clarity of the vision.

One of the best ways to keep your volunteers motivated is to make sure they understand the principle of the chain. (See chapter 4 to review this principle.) People are motivated to serve and continue serving when they see how their service is impacting others for good.

Good Network (GN). Your network refers to your means of getting new people into the ministry system through the promotion structure that supports it. You must be constantly refilling your network—getting people into the lake, as Tim would say—by following up with those who indicate an interest in serving on their connection cards, promoting serving to those who join groups, challenging second-time guests to serve, maintaining an ever-growing list of potential servers, and so on. Encourage people to get involved through preaching, specific challenges, and ministry fairs. However you want to go about it, make sure you are continually getting new people connected. My chiropractor once told me that to grow his practice he followed one simple rule: "The more you greet," he said, "the more you treat." For us, the more people we add to our ministry lake network each week, the healthier our ministry system is going be (okay, so that's not as pithy as my chiropractor's proverb, but you get the point).

All of these elements add up to create a constant influx of new servers. If a volunteer has a good experience, is working within a specific timeline, is challenged to reproduce herself with accountability and motivation, and is supported by a good network that is bringing people into the funnel, she will duplicate herself over time—and then time and time again.

By working to improve each of these five variables, you can increase the number of new volunteers always available to you. Never again will you feel like you need to beg for a volunteer; never again will you feel like a one-person show; never again will you feel like you are overstepping your bounds trying to get someone to serve. Even though we are analyzing this method of constant recruitment and reproduction through the lens of a formula with variables, at its core this process comes down to trusting the Holy Spirit and cooperating with him in connecting people to service for his glory.

The Four Cs of Empowerment

In addition to understanding the formula for reproducing volunteers, you also need to step back and take a macro look at ongoing recruitment from the perspective of what I like to call "The Four Cs of Empowerment"—Clarity, Consideration, Caring, and Courtesy.

Clarity

Clarity is the holy grail of the ministry system. As we have discussed in detail, clarity at every level is key. It is imperative for getting your people to sign up for first-serve opportunities; it's essential for getting them on the ministry ladder; it's critical to their advancement up the ladder. The greatest misconception about communication is that it has taken place. Do everything in your power to make clarity a top priority as you implement your system.

Consideration

How considerate are you of your volunteers? Do you see them as the men and women they are, or do you see them simply as someone who can fill a ministry need? Take care to see your volunteers as people—people with busy schedules and real challenges. If you treat a volunteer like he is just someone who is at your service to run sound or to be an usher or work with kids, without really seeing him and engaging with him for who he is, he will pick up on your lack of consideration. In that case he definitely won't stay around too long, much less recruit anyone else or reproduce himself. See people as people, not just as volunteers.

Caring

Consideration naturally leads to caring. Care for your volunteers by praying for them and keeping in touch with them about the issues and events in their lives. If they need to spend some time talking with you, make time for them. Your servers hold a special position within your church; make sure you care for them accordingly.

Courtesy

Sometimes when people are in a position with expectations attached to it, we forget to be courteous when something goes wrong. Of course, you and I need to hold our volunteers to the agreed-upon expectations of their position agreements and covenants, but that doesn't mean that we don't offer them common courtesy. Offer grace when someone is running late. The same goes if someone is sick for a couple of Sundays. Often, the more actively someone is involved in serving, the more we let simple courtesies slip away. Again, your volunteers do not exist just to fill a role. Treat them with the respect and courtesy they deserve in every situation.

By putting the formula for reproducing volunteers in place and by paying attention to the Four Cs of Empowerment, we can ensure that more and more people will continually be finding their place of service. And if their passion spurs them to wear face paint and costumes while they serve, well . . . okay, that's probably not a good idea. But at least they will be actively engaged in God's purpose for their lives—something that will be enough in and of itself.

10

creating a culture
of celebration

SHOWING GRATITUDE TO PEOPLE WHO SERVE

Celebrate what you want to see more of.

—Tom Peters

They have been a wonderful encouragement to me, as they
have been to you. You must show your appreciation to all
who serve so well.

—1 Corinthians 16:18

Church leaders are focused, driven individuals. We constantly
feel the weight and responsibility of leading the people under
our care well, because we understand that the way we lead
them has eternal ramifications. I'm not saying we don't have

a fun side too—we are filled with the joy of the Lord after all (right?)—but sometimes we get so consumed by daily pressures that we forget to celebrate the incredible things God is doing around us.

I'm certainly guilty of forgetting to celebrate. I tend to forge ahead into the next thing and then the next without slowing down to enjoy the fruit of my labor or the gifts of God. Enter my phenomenal wife. On my birthday last year, Kelley insisted that I take the entire day off. I didn't argue; I knew I needed a break, so I rearranged my schedule and planned to spend the day with my family.

When I walked into the kitchen to pour myself a cup of coffee on my birthday morning, a bulky, square card was resting against the coffeepot. The front of the card simply said "Happy Birthday!" But when I opened it up, Kool & The Gang's "Celebration" blasted out of the cardboard. As my son started dancing around the kitchen to "Celebrate good times, come on!" I got the point. Kelley wanted me to take a day to celebrate the blessings in my life.

Now I keep that birthday card on a shelf in my office to remind me that I need to celebrate good times! And so do you. In the church, we simply don't celebrate enough. Consider Nehemiah's words:

> Go and celebrate with a feast of rich foods and sweet drinks, and share gifts of food with people who have nothing prepared. This is a sacred day before our Lord. Don't be dejected and sad, for the joy of the LORD is your strength! (Neh. 8:10)

Throughout the Bible, God goes so far as to command his people to celebrate. There's always a festival going on or some other occasion to rejoice and have a little fun. Jesus was always going to parties. He modeled celebration for us by taking frequent opportunities to joyfully acknowledge the work of his Father. So who are we to plow ahead without proper celebration?

While there are countless scenarios, events, and people to celebrate in your church, learning to celebrate your volunteers and their service is key to growing and maintaining a healthy minis-try system. Celebration is a reward. When you celebrate someone who has served, or celebrate a specific step a volunteer has taken, you are rewarding her for her service. Not to mention, what gets rewarded gets repeated. This is true in your marriage, with your kids, with your friends—and with the volunteers in your church. When people feel underappreciated, they pull away. When you reward them, they flourish—and they work to please you again in the same way. You will get more of what you celebrate.

What gets rewarded gets repeated.

Celebrate Good Times

As your volunteers step into and move through your ministry system, there are specific points at which you should plan to celebrate their service. Let's take a look at six key times of celebration:

1. When a Volunteer Serves for the First Time. In part 1 we dissected the details of providing new servers with first-serve opportunities. When a volunteer or a group of volunteers takes that first step, celebrate it. For instance, when a small group shows up at a Sunday service to serve together for the first time, point them out and make a big deal about them being there. Have everyone give a cheer for these new volunteers.

At The Journey, when new people come to Super Service Thursday, we create an atmosphere of celebration around them. As the night draws to an end, we high-five them and tell them how great it is that they decided to volunteer. We make them feel good about getting involved. When a new volunteer serves on the worship arts team for the first time, we applaud her at the end of the day. She is a hero for stepping into that first-serve opportunity, so we celebrate with her. You get the picture: whenever people volunteer for the first time, notice and celebrate their first step with them. What gets rewarded gets repeated. (Visit www.ChurchLeader Insights.com/connect for downloadable emails that we use to say "thank you" to people who serve.)

"Thanks for hanging out longer than usual today, Tim," David says as the two men slide on their jackets and head for the door. "Can't believe my little joke about feeling like a one-man show led to such a great discussion. Honestly, I've never thought of approaching the whole volunteer issue the way we've been talking about today."

"No problem," Tim answers. "This is an area that took me quite awhile to figure out. I'm happy to pass along any help I can."

As David and Tim walk through the front of the diner and out the door, Tim notices that the tables are now full of happy customers. The crowd at the hostess's stand is gone. He sees a couple of servers who weren't there before taking down orders. Things seem to be back to normal, running smoothly.

Tim reaches into his pocket for his keys and accidentally pulls out a 3x5 index card with them. David notices that the card has a few names scribbled on it.

"What's that?" David asks.

"Oh," Tim says with a chuckle. "I meant to leave this at the office last night, but I forgot so I stuck it back in my pocket this morning. Just as well, because it reminds me of something else to mention to you."

"Nice! A bonus tip to mull over on my drive," David says.

"You know how I said it's really important to thank your volunteers when they serve for the first time?"

"Yep, sure do," David answers.

"Well, that's what this note card is for. Every Sunday, I carry a note card like this in my pocket. When I meet someone who's serving for the first time, I write his or her name down on the card. Then, on Monday or Tuesday, I shoot a quick email to those new volunteers to let them know I noticed their service and to congratulate them on taking the first step." Tim holds the card up for David to see. "So, these are the names of Sunday's first-time volunteers."

"What a great idea," David says. "I bet it catches them off guard to get an email from the pastor—in a good way!"

"That's my hope. I also use the email as a chance to cast some vision for the area where they were serving or for the church in general."

"Good thinking. That will bring them a little further on board."

"Exactly. Now, I don't meet everyone who serves for the first time every week and I don't always send the email when I do, but I've found that, as much as possible, this is a really effective habit to get into."

"Wow. I'm glad you had that little note card in your pocket, Tim." David laughs.

"Ah, meant to be, I guess," Tim says. "I can tell you, it definitely resonates with people and makes them want to come back and serve again. Give it a try." Tim opens his car door and glances at his watch. "Alright, David. Great breakfast! Same time, same place next month?"

"You bet! See you then, Tim," David says. "Thanks for everything."

As Tim pulls away, David unlocks his own car door. He can hardly wait to get back to the office to start working on some of what he and Tim talked about today. He can feel it—the days of being a one-man show are about to be over for good.

---

2. When a Volunteer Reaches a Service Milestone. Celebrate when someone completes a significant term of service. Significant doesn't necessarily equate with long; it simply denotes a period of time that could be considered a milestone. For example, if someone has served in children's ministry for six months, recognize her. If someone has been part of the worship arts team for one year, recognize that milestone. To clarify, this doesn't mean they haven't taken a break during that time period. The principle of stress and release always applies. We are simply recognizing people who are enthusiastically engaged in serving, take their proper time away, and then continue with their service.

At The Journey we have formalized this celebration for group leaders. Every semester, at group leader training, we publicly recognize and celebrate the people who have been leading groups for a significant period of time. We ask the people who have been leading for a year to stand, and we celebrate them. Then we ask the people who have been leading for three years to stand, and we celebrate them. You get the idea. When we get to the people in the room who have been leading the longest, we invite them up front, talk to them about their experience serving, and celebrate them in a big way. You get more of what you celebrate. (For links to the software we use to track this, visit www.ChurchLeader Insights.com/connect.)

3. When a Volunteer Moves Up a Rung on the Ministry Ladder. Recognize your volunteers when they climb to a new level on the ministry ladder. You don't need to make the recognition elaborate or complicated; keep it simple. If you have a new team leader at your team leaders meeting, just make it a point to acknowledge her and have everyone welcome her. If you have someone who has stepped into a leadership position at the Sunday service, make sure everyone serving knows it. Be aware; never miss an opportunity to celebrate the growth of your people.

4. During a Weekend Service. Celebrating your volunteers during the worship service can be powerful. Here are three ways to celebrate (and encourage, by default) ministry every week:

- **Pray for your volunteers.** Praying for your volunteers in your worship services will help create a culture of volunteerism within your church. When you step onto the stage, or into the pulpit, for your premessage prayer, pray for the people who are serving. Pray something along the lines of, "God, before we go any further in the service, we thank you for the volunteers who are serving in our children's area today. We pray your blessing on them." It never hurts to make a little joke about helping them keep the kids under control too. Levity is good.

  Each week, pray for a different segment of volunteers. You may want to jot down a rotation schedule in the front of your Bible. For example, the first Sunday of the month, you pray for the children's workers; the second Sunday, you pray for the people who serve in your small groups ministry; the third, you pray for the volunteers at the Sunday service and those who come early to set things up; the fourth Sunday, you pray for all of the people who volunteer at your office during the week, preparing everything for the weekend service. The spirit of ministry that these simple prayers will create in your church will surprise you.

- **Praise your volunteers.** When you see people serving, thank them. Say an encouraging word and give them a high five. Pat them on the back. Take every opportunity you can to praise your volunteers for their service.

- **Ask volunteers to give a testimony.** Invite some of your volunteers to give a testimony about how they have grown through serving, during a Sunday service. When your congregation sees someone they know step onstage and give a testimony about the significance serving brings to his or her life, they will be more eager to get connected.

Remember Stuart? You know, the high-powered investment broker who served so faithfully at Super Service Thursday? (See chapter 3 for Stuart's story.) I will never forget the time we invited Stuart to give his testimony during a Sunday service. He stood onstage and painted an incredible word picture for his listeners. He told them about the work he did, the international cities he visited, and the luxurious hotels he was blessed to stay in. Then he told them that, as much as possible, he orchestrated his schedule to be in town on Thursday nights so he could serve at Super Service Thursday. He said that being involved in the process of growing the kingdom was the most significant part of his week, and he didn't want to miss it. As Stuart was wrapping up, he mentioned that the people he served alongside had become like family to him. Wow.

Testimonies are a powerful tool for touching people's hearts and spurring them to action.

Stories of service attract new people to service. They don't have to be grand stories like Stuart's—they can be simple testimonies speaking to the impact that serving has had on someone's life. Testimonies are a powerful tool for touching people's hearts and spurring them to action.

5. *When a Volunteer Is Not Expecting It.* Pop quiz for the married men: When is the best time to buy flowers for your

wife? If you thought, "When she's least expecting them," then you probably have a happy marriage. In the same way, the single best time to reward a volunteer through celebration is when he is not expecting it. A surprise gesture of appreciation stays with someone much longer than an expected one.

Many years ago, our pastor of worship arts, Jason, started something that we have been using at The Journey ever since. He had about a hundred people scheduled to go through an upcoming worship arts orientation meeting. The purpose of the meeting was to bring everyone who had recently connected to worship arts together to go over what it meant to be part of the worship arts team and have everyone sign the covenant. As the attendees arrived for the meeting, Jason had them check in by filling out a form that asked for their name, email, and mailing address. The form also posed a couple of arbitrary questions, like "What's your favorite flavor of ice cream?"

About six months later—after everyone who attended the meeting had forgotten about that form and the questions they answered—Jason picked a random week to surprise some of his recent volunteers. He pulled together the names of everyone on his team who had served the previous Sunday and sent each of those volunteers a $5 Cold Stone Creamery gift card. He attached a note to each gift card referencing that individual's favorite ice cream flavor. He wrote things like, "Dear Joe, Thanks for serving with worship arts on Sunday. Have some Rocky Road on us!" The volunteers who received Jason's unexpected gesture were thrilled—and shocked. They couldn't figure out how Jason had known all of their favorite ice cream flavors. A little planning goes a long way. (For more on how Jason and I have structured the worship ministries at The Journey, see the book we wrote together: *Engage: A Guide to Creating Life-Transforming Worship Services*, by Nelson Searcy and Jason Hatley, with Jennifer Dykes Henson [Baker, 2011].)

We make it a point to reward our small group leaders in a similar way. When we have leaders training, we ask them all kinds of crazy questions and then put their answers on file. On random days throughout the year, we'll sit down and write a few unexpected thank-you notes, often including a reference to something they've shared with us. We usually have everyone on staff take ten minutes to write three or four notes, so the process doesn't take too much time out of anyone's day. Receiving this kind of surprise celebration lets people know that their service is noticed and appreciated—which makes them feel great and makes them want to keep serving. What gets rewarded gets repeated.

The danger to watch out for with something random is that it can continually be pushed off. To avoid procrastinating on our unexpected celebrations, I go through my calendar at the beginning of every year and note five or six days during the upcoming twelve months when we will surprise our volunteers with a reward. One of those days, we may choose to write notes to children's ministry workers, another our Sunday servers, another our worship arts volunteers, and another our group leaders. Let me encourage you to follow the same gratitude strategy in every ministry area of your church.

6. *Anytime!* While the five points of celebration mentioned above are important, don't limit yourself to them exclusively.

Take every opportunity you see to celebrate your volunteers and their service to the kingdom. Celebrate good times! The fruit of celebration is well worth the effort it takes to build it into your system.

How to Thank Volunteers

As you can already tell, thanking your volunteers is a key element of celebrating them. Really, thanking your people well is the *best* way of celebrating them. One of my greatest mentors throughout my years of ministry has been Steve Stroope, lead pastor of Lake Pointe Church near Dallas, Texas, and author of the fantastic book *Tribal Church* (Broadman & Holman, 2012). Steve has a unique grasp on the importance of how we as church leaders should thank those who serve alongside us. He has influenced me a great deal in this area. So, with courtesy to Steve, let's take a look at a few of the most effective ways of thanking your volunteers:

- **Money**: Everyone appreciates being thanked with money. Essentially, that's how we are rewarding people when we give them a Cold Stone Creamery gift card. Even millionaires welcome a free ice cream, a $5 Starbucks card, or a $10 gas card. If you build these small tokens of gratitude into your system, you will be saying "thank you" in a language that everyone understands and appreciates.

- **Private Praise and/or Public Praise**: Part of your job is to determine how your people like to be praised. When it comes to private versus public praise, people are strikingly different. In my experience, most people love private praise. They drink it in. There's nothing like a one-on-one conversation where you look someone in the eye, tell him how much he means to you and to the church, and remind him that he is making a difference. Such a thank-you goes a long way.

Public praise can also be extremely effective, but you have to be more careful when issuing it. Many people absolutely abhor public praise. While they appreciate a private word of encouragement, being pointed out in public embarrasses them. Other people, however, beam under the spotlight of public acknowledgment. Pay attention to your volunteers and do your best to determine what kind of praise they would most like to receive.

- **Access**: You may not realize it, but access to you and your key leaders is important to many of your volunteers. Having the opportunity to sit down over a cup of coffee with you may be all the thanks some of them need. Knowing they can shoot you an email that will be answered quickly makes them feel important and appreciated. You may have a hard time acknowledging that someone might see access to you as a gift, but it's the truth. Access is a great way to thank certain volunteers.

- **Input**: People feel a stronger connection to decisions and situations that they speak into. So giving your volunteers a chance to have input into certain goings on around your church is an effective way to thank them for their service. For example, recently I was preparing for a message series on worship. As part of my research, I went to our key worship arts volunteers and asked them, "What are your biggest questions and concerns about worship?" A few weeks later, when I began the series, these volunteers would hear a reference to something they had mentioned and feel like they'd had input into the series. As a result, they felt valued.

Similarly, if you have a problem in a ministry area and are having a hard time finding a solution, ask the people who serve in that area to help you. Invite them to stay fifteen minutes late one day, explain the situation to them, and see what kind of answers they come up with. You may be surprised that they give you the exact solution you couldn't pinpoint on your own.

There's no problem in the kingdom that can't be solved with the right people in the room. Unfortunately, as leaders, we are often hesitant to admit when we need help figuring out how to get from point A to point B. But when we reach out to other leaders and allow them to have input, we create a huge amount of buy-in. Having their voices heard gives volunteers ownership. And as we all know, people taking ownership of their faith and their place of service is essential to our mission.

- **Knowledge**: Okay, time for a cliché—*knowledge is power.* Not only that, but thanking your volunteers by providing them with some inside knowledge of the church is powerful. (I'd say we just took that cliché and made it better.)

In our structure at The Journey, we have something called "Focus Time" before each service. A few minutes before worship begins, we pull everyone together, intentionally shift our focus from the bustle of setup to what's about to happen in the service, and pray over the upcoming hour. During focus time, we give our volunteers an inside peek into the church. We tell them something no one else knows. It may be something as simple as how many people we have signed up to be baptized at the next baptism, or it may be a tidbit of information from the previous week's staff meeting. Nothing major—just a little something to give those volunteers a sense of seeing behind the curtain.

Imparting privileged knowledge to your volunteers makes them feel trusted and respected. It's a terrific way to say thank you. Not to mention, it gives you the opportunity to plant seeds with these leaders about upcoming announcements and events. When everyone else finds out, your volunteers will already be in the know and will have already bought in, which will create a greater atmosphere of excitement throughout the rest of the church.

- **Significance**: Thank your volunteers by reminding them how significant their service is. This mode of thanks ties back, again, to the principle of the chain. Continually remind your volunteers of the connection between their ministry and the eternity of the people they are serving. Without the sound guys, no one could hear the message of the gospel. Without the ushers, people wouldn't have a smooth welcome experience and would not be as open to God's leading during the service. Make sure your volunteers know how important they are; for many of them, that's all the thanks they need.

171

- **Excellence**: Provide your volunteers with the tools they need to perform their responsibilities with excellence. I'm not suggesting that you run out and buy new cameras and new kids supplies to thank your volunteers; simply that, within reason, you make sure that you are giving your volunteers the best resources you can, so they can do their jobs the best that they can.

(For more from Steve Stroope and to see other recommended resources, visit www.ChurchLeaderInsights.com/connect.)

A small tweak in the way you celebrate your volunteers has the potential to reap big rewards for your overall ministry system. Remember, we are dealing with people who are willingly giving of themselves. They are sacrificing their own time in an effort to make someone else's more meaningful. Heeding Jesus's imperative to serve—shaped by how you've taught and led them—they are pouring themselves out for the growth of the church and the glory of God. Celebrate these men and women. Love them; care for them; thank them. What gets rewarded gets repeated.

conclusion

If you keep on doing what you've always done, you'll keep on getting what you've always got.

—W. L. Bateman

Commit your actions to the LORD, and your plans will succeed.

—Proverbs 16:3

All good things take time. Helping people connect, find their place on the right ministry ladder, and mature into fully developing followers of Jesus is an ongoing project—one you will be working on from now until the day you hang up your hat. Likewise, growing the ministries and people in your church to the God-honoring level you envision for them will take concerted effort on your part. But that's a good thing! God never promises that shepherding and shaping our people into his image will be easy. It will, however, be well worth the effort when we see previously disconnected individuals find their sweet spot of service and come alive as servants of Jesus Christ.

The ultimate goal of the ministry system is to create a church full of eager volunteers who take Paul's words from Philippians 2 to heart as they follow Jesus's example of selflessness:

> Don't be selfish; don't try to impress others. Be humble, thinking of others as better than yourselves. Don't look out only for your own interests, but take an interest in others, too. You must have the same attitude that Christ Jesus had. Though he was God, he did not think of equality with God as something to cling to. Instead, he gave up his divine privileges; he took the humble position of a slave and was born as a human being. When he appeared in human form, he humbled himself in obedience to God and died a criminal's death on a cross. Therefore, God elevated him to the place of highest honor and gave him the name above all other names, that at the name of Jesus every knee should bow, in heaven and on earth and under the earth, and every tongue confess that Jesus Christ is Lord, to the glory of God the Father. (Phil. 2:3–11)

That's what you want, right? You want a congregation of humble servants who look out for the interests of others over their own; a church filled with people who have the same servant attitude Jesus had. And that's exactly what you should have. God's church is not meant to be lacking. Instead, it should be fully resourced and able to operate at the height of its redemptive potential. Your church should be vibrant and healthy, teeming with volunteers every week. That's God's vision—and my prayer—for you.

Getting Started

So where do you start? Well, to answer that question, let's visit with a professor I've become quite fond of. You may have met this professor before. In fact, if you've read my books *Ignite: How to Spark Immediate Growth in Your Church* (Baker, 2009), *Maximize: How to Develop Extravagant Givers in Your Church* (Baker, 2010), and/or *Engage: A Guide to Creating Life-Transforming Worship Services* (Baker, 2011), I know you have met him; he lends his insight to all three. The professor is worth visiting with again here. Let's peer into his classroom, this time through the lens of the ministry system.

Once there was a wise professor who set out to prove a point to a bunch of sleepy students. One morning, he walked into his classroom with a big, widemouthed jar under his arm. He made his way to the front of the room and set the jar on his desk. With the students paying little attention, he filled the jar with five big stones. He put the stones in one by one until the jar couldn't hold anymore. Then he asked his students, "Is this jar full?" They half-nodded their assertion that it was.

The professor pulled a bucket of pebbles from under his desk. Slowly, he poured the pebbles into the jar. They bounced and settled into the small spaces that had been created between the stones. Once again, the professor asked his students, who were now slightly more awake, "Is this jar full?" They all quietly contended that, yes, of course it was.

The professor proceeded to pull another bucket from beneath his desk—this one filled with fine sand. As the students looked on, he tilted the bucket of sand into the jar. The granules quickly filled in the barely visible cracks and crevices left between the stones and pebbles. This time, when asked, "Is this jar full?" the class answered with a resounding, "Yes!"

In response to his students' certainty, the professor reached under his desk and brought out a pitcher of water. The students watched in amazement as the professor poured the entire pitcher into the jar.

Now, the professor asked a different question, "What was the point of this illustration? What was I trying to teach you through this now-full jar?"

A student in the back called out, "You were showing us that you can always fit more things into your life if you really work at it?"

"No," replied the professor. "The point is that you have to put the big rocks in first, or you'll never get them in."

The Big Rocks

When it comes to doubling your volunteer base, there are three big rocks you need to put in place as quickly as possible. These three rocks won't propel the system to effectiveness on their own, but you must get them in place before you start trying to move ahead with the details. Once you get these elements in the jar, other pieces of the system will fill in the empty spaces and gaps around them.

If you can't do everything suggested in these pages right away, focus on getting the big rocks set. Without them, nothing else we've discussed will be useful and, with them, you will be leaps and bounds ahead of where you are now. Here are the three big rocks and what you can do immediately to start getting them into position.

Rock #1: Clarified Theology of Ministry
Immediate Action Step: Sit down with your team, if you haven't already, and talk through your theology of ministry in detail. Answer the questions I posed to you at the close of chapter 2. Nail down what you believe about the importance of serving and how those beliefs play out in your church.

Rock #2: 30/50/20 Rule
Immediate Action Step: The 30/50/20 Rule holds that, ideally, you should have 30 percent of your church in the pre-serving stage, 50 percent of your church actively serving for at least one hour per week, and 20 percent involved in evangelism. What are your current percentages? Compared to the ideal, determine where you are and set an immediate, achievable goal. Maybe your first goal is just to raise your percentage of active volunteers from 5 percent to 10 percent, or from 10 percent to 20 percent. Wherever you are right now is okay—acknowledge it and set a new benchmark to work toward. Pray right now for God to double your volunteer base over the next twelve months. Study this book with your team and then pray again for God to continue doubling your volunteer base until you have at least 30 percent of your people serving one hour a week or more.

Rock #3: Celebration Mindset
Immediate Action Step: Don't wait to celebrate. Start celebrating your current volunteers now. Celebration leads to reproduction, which means that new people will want to get involved in serving, which means that you'll need to introduce them to new or current serving opportunities, which means that they'll soon want to step up on the ministry ladder

they are best suited for, which means you'll have a chance to celebrate their progress, which means. . . . See how it all ties together?

The Pebbles

Here are a few smaller pebbles that can help you close some of the gaps between the big rocks right away. Take a look at these three little things that you can begin doing now to boost the level of volunteerism in your church. Combined with the immediate action steps mentioned above, these will give you a quick start toward putting the structure in place to recruit and grow lots of volunteers:

1. **Put a 3x5 Index Card in Your Pocket**: This Sunday, put a blank note card in your pocket and, as you see them, write down the names of people you can celebrate with an email or a handwritten thank-you note this week.
2. **Practice the Big Ask**: Identify a need in your church and create a onetime event to meet that need. Personally call and email a few people and ask them to serve at the onetime event. Remember to choose your words carefully.
3. **Sketch Out Your First Ministry Ladder**: Pick one area of your church and start defining its ministry ladder. How many rungs will the ladder have? What expectations sit on what rungs? Working through the process of building your first ministry ladder will help to solidify many of the concepts we've discussed and will make building the rest of your ladders much easier.

CANEI

Constant **A**nd **N**ever **E**nding **I**mprovement

Perhaps most important, as you move forward with putting your ministry system in place, embrace the principle of CANEI. CANEI stands for Constant And Never Ending Improvement. You may not be able to take all of the steps we've discussed right away. That's okay. Do what you can as you can, and continually strive for CANEI. As Napoleon Hill once said, "Do not wait; the time will never be 'just right.' Start where you stand, and work with whatever tools you may have at your command, and better tools will be found as you go along."[10] You have powerful tools at your command now; go ahead and get started. Just think: if you make only a 1 percent improvement to your ministry system every week, in two years it will be 100 percent better than it is now.

On the other hand, if you are ready to forge ahead with the details of the system you have discovered here and you meet with great success in short order, I still implore you to always remember the principle of CANEI. No matter how many volunteers you have, or how strong and effective your ministry system becomes, don't ever get comfortable. Always be on the lookout for ways to improve—for ways to connect even more people even more effectually. Excellence, after all, is a goal that keeps moving higher the closer we get to it.

Servants are not created overnight. But by implementing what you have learned in these pages, while seeking the continual guidance of the Holy Spirit, you can put a ministry system into action that will produce an abundance of volunteers in your church. Never again will you be lacking; never again will you be a one-person show. Even more important, you will have the awesome joy of seeing people become more like Jesus as they connect to your church, to other believers, and to God's ultimate plan for their lives through service. What a responsibility; what a calling. May we never take it lightly.

postscript

I hope this book will become a conversation starter between us. I am constantly developing resources and gathering ideas from others to help you lead a fully resourced church. In fact, I recently held a private event for my coaching alumni where I taught everything I know about a healthy ministry (it would fill at least three books like this one) called *The Ministry Intensive*. You can find information about securing the recording of this intensive event at *Connect*'s website:

www.ChurchLeaderInsights.com/connect

You can also use the website to connect with me. I would love to hear your story and to continue discussing the ways we can grow together for God's glory.

Your partner in ministry,
Nelson Searcy
Lead Pastor, The Journey Church
Founder, www.ChurchLeaderInsights.com

notes

Chapter 1 The Significance of Service

1. Mother Teresa, quoted on Soulful Tributes, www.soulfultributes. org/spiritual_figures/mother_teresa/biography.

Chapter 4 The Power of New Beginnings

2. Robert Collier, *Riches within Your Reach!* (New York: Jeremy P. Tarcher, 1947), 151.

3. John Milton, quoted on QOTD, www.qotd.org/search/search. html?aid=1742.

4. Tony Morgan and Tim Stevens, *Simply Strategic Volunteers: Empowering People for Ministry* (Loveland, CO: Group, 2005), 188.

Chapter 5 Igniting Involvement

5. Bill Hybels, *The Volunteer Revolution: Unleashing the Power of Everybody* (Grand Rapids: Zondervan, 2004), 13–14.

6. Wayne Cordeiro, *Doing Church as a Team* (Ventura, CA: Regal, 2004), 19.

Chapter 6 Lake and Ladders

7. Rick Warren, *The Purpose Driven Church: Growth without Compromising Your Message & Mission* (Grand Rapids: Zondervan, 1995), 371.

Chapter 8 Calling Out the Called

8. C. H. Spurgeon, *Lectures to My Students* (Grand Rapids: Zondervan, 1972), 18, 39.

Chapter 9 Ongoing Recruitment and Reproduction

9. Saint Augustine, quoted on Servants of the Pierced Hearts of Jesus and Mary, www.piercedhearts.org/theology_heart/life_saints/augustine. htm.

Conclusion

10. Napoleon Hill, quoted on Quotation Collection, www.quotation-collection.com/author/Napoleon_Hill/quotes.

appendices

journey membership covenant

Note that to be a member at The Journey you must commit to serve. We follow up quarterly with our members to confirm their volunteer involvement.

Membership Covenant

- I will protect the unity of my church.
  - . . . by acting in love toward other members
  - . . . by refusing to gossip
  - . . . by following the leaders
- I will share the responsibility of my church.
  - . . . by praying for its growth
  - . . . by inviting the unchurched to attend
  - . . . by warmly welcoming those who visit
- I will serve the ministry of my church.
  - . . . by discovering my gifts and talents
  - . . . by being equipped to serve by my pastors
  - . . . by developing a servant's heart
- I will support the testimony of my church.
  - . . . by attending faithfully
  - . . . by living a godly life
  - . . . by giving regularly

Signature _____

Date _____

journey growth group covenant

THE JOURNEY
Growth Group Covenant

Welcome to Growth Groups at The Journey. Congratulations on your desire to grow deeper in your relationship with God through this weekly study and the relationships that will begin in this Growth Group.

As a member of this group, you will be asked to enter into a covenant with the other members to make this Growth Group a priority. To be a part of the group, you are asked to make the following commitments:

1. I will make this group a priority by attending each week, keeping up with my assignments, and participating in group discussion.

2. I will regularly attend The Journey services and contribute to the ministry of the church through my attendance, giving, service, and inviting of others.

3. I will strive to build authentic relationships with those in this group by showing care, providing encouragement, and praying for their needs.

4. I will serve together with my group once a month during the semester and will participate in a mission project and play together with my group at least once.

I will explore honestly my next steps for spiritual growth.

_____   _____
Name   Date

For a free downloadable version of this covenant, see www. ChurchLeaderInsights.com/connect.

journey growth group leader covenant

In the covenant below, note that serving is part of the commitment to participate in a small group:

THE JOURNEY
Growth Group Leader Covenant

Thank you for serving as a Growth Group leader at The Journey. As a Growth Group leader, you will be viewed by those in your group as a leader in the church. As a result, we ask that you enter into covenant with the other Growth Group leaders by making the following commitments:

1. I will embody and reflect the values and principles of The Journey and will follow the leadership of the staff team.
2. I will faithfully attend The Journey on Sundays and:
   - Intentionally identify and greet those in my Growth Group.
   - Participate in the church through my financial giving.
   - Lead my group in serving together once a month.
3. I will make my Growth Group a priority by:
   - Faithfully attending my Growth Group.
   - Preparing beforehand for my group each week.
   - Inviting/welcoming others to join my group.
4. I understand that I am responsible for the care of my Growth Group. As a result, I will:
   - Pray for the individuals in my group.
   - Follow up with each person in my group.
   - Lead my group in providing care for one another.
5. I will strive to create an environment of growth in my group by:
   - Involving as many people as possible in group discussion.
   - Creating a safe, comfortable, and welcoming environment.
   - Beginning and ending on time.

_____   _____
Name   Date

For a free downloadable version of this covenant, see www
.ChurchLeaderInsights.com/connect.

journey growth group
team leader covenant

Note that as someone moves up the ladder to a team leader, the expectations on serving, giving, and membership increase:

THE JOURNEY
Growth Group Team Leader Covenant

Thank you for serving as a Growth Group team leader at The Journey. For a team leader there are expectations and responsibilities that go beyond those of a Growth Group leader. As such, you will be viewed as one of the key leaders of The Journey's Growth Groups.

As a Growth Group team leader, you are asked to enter into covenant with the other team leaders to make this ministry area a priority. To be a team leader, you are asked to make the following commitments:

1. I will embody and reflect the values of The Journey and will follow the leadership of the staff team. This includes:
   - Striving to live a godly life.
   - Attending Sunday services regularly.
   - Honoring God with my finances by tithing.
2. I understand that I am responsible for the care of the Growth Group leaders who are assigned to me. As a result, I will:
   - Pray for each of them daily.
   - Personally contact each of them weekly.
   - Meet with my team together once a semester (GG Huddle).
3. I will make attending monthly team leader meetings a priority.
4. Each semester I will assist my Growth Group coach in recruiting new Growth Group leaders and in setting up new Growth Groups.
5. I will assist with Growth Group preparation, promotion, and programs when possible (for example, GG Leaders Training, Growth Group Table, etc.).

_____   _____

Name   Date

For a free downloadable version of this covenant, see www
.ChurchLeaderInsights.com/connect.

first-time server opportunities

Here's a sample of first-time server opportunities that are available at one of our campuses:

First-Time Server—Opportunities

- Setup Team—Upper West Side
  —Arrive at 7:00 am to unload truck and vans. Will attend the 10:00 am service. (4 people)
  —Arrive at 8:00 am to set up tables and pipe and drape. Will attend the 10:00 am service. (4 people)
- Teardown Team—Upper West Side
  —Arrive at 2:00 pm to tear down tables and pipe and drape. Will attend the 1:00 pm service. (6 people)
  —Arrive at 2:00 pm to load truck and vans. Will attend the 1:00 pm service. (6 people)
- 10:00 am Service
  —Usher (6 people)
  —Offering (6 people)
  —Program Distributor (2 to 4 people)
  —Front Door Greeter (6 people)
  —Resource Table Greeter (4 people)
  —Info Table Greeter (2 people)
- 11:30 am Service
  —Usher (6 people)
  —Offering (6 people)

- —Program Distributor (2 to 4 people)
- —Front Door Greeter (6 people)
- —Resource Table Greeter (4 people)
- —Info Table Greeter (2 people)
- 1:00 pm Service
  - —Usher (6 people)
  - —Offering (6 people)
  - —Program Distributor (2 to 4 people)
  - —Front Door Greeter (6 people)
  - —Resource Table Greeter (4 people)
  - —Info Table Greeter (2 people)
- Setup Team—The Village
  - —Arrive at 4:00 pm to unload truck and vans. (2 people)
  - —Arrive at 5:00 pm to set up tables. (2 people)
- Teardown Team—The Village
  - —Meet staff member after the 6:30 pm service to tear down and load equipment into The Journey truck and vans. (4 people)
- 6:30 pm Service
  - —Usher (6 people)
  - —Offering (6 people)
  - —Program Distributor (2 to 4 people)
  - —Front Door Greeter (4 people)
  - —Resource Table Greeter (3 people)
  - —Info Table Greeter (2 people)

serving at the journey

Following is what we say about our serving philosophy on our website:

Serving is a great way to grow in your relationship with God, show God's love to others, and to demonstrate the attitude that Jesus modeled when he walked on earth. God created each of us with specific talents and gifts to use in impacting others. Our goal is to provide a place for you to invest yourself serving in the church. Get involved serving this week. In giving of yourself you'll find significance you never imagined!

Check out the following serving opportunities at The Journey:

Journey Kidz Team
Worship Arts Team
Serving on Sunday

For we are God's workmanship, created in Christ Jesus to do good works, which God prepared in advance for us to do. (Eph. 2:10)

serving on sunday

Following is the copy we use on The Journey's website to encourage people to sign up for serving:

Sign Up to Serve

Take your worship experience to a new level by serving this Sunday @ The Journey!

Here are three great ways you can serve:

1) Serve on the First Impressions Team

When you walk into The Journey on Sunday, who is the first person you see? A greeter welcoming you? An usher handing you a program or helping you find a seat? The people that make The Journey Sunday service a great experience from the time you walk in the door are people just like you. They come a little early and help make sure that Sundays at The Journey are great . . . and you can too!

By serving on the first impressions team, you will impact hundreds of attenders, meet new people, and have a great time!

Time Requirement: Arrive to the service at 9:30 am and meet our front of house coordinator in the lobby.

2) Serve on the Front of House Setup Team

What do you experience when you walk into the lobby of The Journey's meeting location each Sunday? Signs to help people find their way, well-organized resources and information on the resource table, music playing, and an area that's been prepared especially for you (and each person who attends that day).

By serving on the front of house setup team, you can help create that welcoming and helpful environment while getting to know other people just like you!

Time Requirement: Arrive to the service at 8:30 am and meet our front of house coordinator in the lobby.

3) Serve on the General Setup Team

Because our church is portable and we meet in a school, each Sunday a group of Journey attenders assists in setting up and tearing down signs, equipment, resources, and more for our church services.

The general setup team is the "special forces" of The Journey that make things happen each Sunday!

Time Requirement: Arrive to the service at 7:30 am and meet our setup coordinator in front of the theater at the high school.

Sign Up to Serve Today!

Complete the form in the gray box on this page to learn more about serving at The Journey.

Want More Info?

Submit the form below for more information about volunteering to serve in one of these exciting areas:

First Name:
Last Name:

Email:
Phone:

I am interested in serving in the following areas:
   __ First Impressions Team (usher, greeter, etc.)
   __ Front of House Setup/Teardown Team
   __ General Setup/Teardown Team

worship arts team serving opportunities

Discover how to use your gifts through one of The Journey's most creative and fun teams—the worship arts team!

The Journey Loves Artists!

So much so that it is our desire to see every artist use their gifts to become all that God has intended for them to be.

The worship arts team at The Journey is a community of artists who, together, unleash the arts to create transformational moments in people's lives. The worship arts team includes visual artists, musicians, dancers, film producers, writers, technicians, actors, and those with a passion for the arts. We believe that God has given us the arts so that we can honor him and share his love with others.

The Worship Arts Team Is a Place To . . .

- **Belong**: build healthy relationships and be a part of something bigger than yourself.
- **Create**: use your God-given talents to serve and do what you were made to do.
- **Become**: discover God's amazing love—and become all that God intends for you to be as an artist.

Get Involved!

If you would like to start using your talents at The Journey, it's easy to get involved. Simply **sign up today.**

- **Band**: The band is made up of instrumentalists (from drums and bass to violins and cellos) who bring the Sunday service worship experience to life.
- **Dance Team**: For dancers of all genres, the dance team choreographs and performs pieces that move and inspire.
- **Design Team**: The design team is made up of graphic, industrial, set, and interior designers as well as illustrators and visual artists who work in the areas of fine art, such as painting, photography, sculpting, and more. The design team creates the exciting visual environment of The Journey's Sunday services.
- **Drama Team**: Whether you're a seasoned professional or a growing actor, the drama team performs quality drama that entertains, encourages introspection, and effectively communicates the message being delivered.
- **Production Team**: The production team is responsible for media and technical production at The Journey. Made up of camera operators, editors, and journalists; sound, light, and video engineers; stage and set crew, the production team is open to all levels of experience and expertise.
- **Vocal Team**: The vocal team is for those who love to sing in a small ensemble and lead worship at the Sunday services with energy and enthusiasm.

- **Writing Team:** The writing team is made up of writers of all backgrounds, including journalism, script, poetry, and screenplay, and it is responsible for writing for various Journey stage and screen productions.

For more information, or to set up an audition, complete the Worship Arts Team Interest Form.

journey kidz serving opportunities

Journey Kidz Team

- Do you want to make a difference in the lives of children?
- Do you have a heart for sharing the gospel with kids?
- If you care about kids and have a desire to work with them, this is the ministry for you!

As a Journey Kidz volunteer, you can choose which age group (nursery, preschool, or elementary) you would like to serve in based on your strengths and talents.

Time Requirement: Two Sundays a month over the course of a four-month semester (January–April, May–August, and September–December).

The next Journey Kidz Overview is coming up soon!

This overview is your opportunity to learn more about serving in Journey Kidz, including volunteer expectations, our mission/values, and what happens on Sundays. Before serving in Kidz, you're required to attend an overview meeting and pass a background check.

To get plugged in, sign up for the next overview using the form below, email Pastor Tommy, or give us a call at . . .

Name:
Email Address:
Phone:

How long have you been attending The Journey?

I am currently . . . I am interested in serving . . .
  in the Nursery (Birth–2 years)
  in Preschool (3–5 years)
  in Elementary (Kindergarten–5th grade)

Sign me up for the next Journey Kidz Overview!
Please let me know when the next overview is scheduled!

community service opportunities

It's not hard to see the needs surrounding us every day. But together, we can make a difference! At The Journey, we believe God has called each of us to serve. That's why we're committed to making a difference in our city and having fun while we do it!

If you are generous with the hungry and start giving yourselves to the down-and-out, your lives will begin to glow in the darkness, your shadowed lives will be bathed in sunlight. (Isa. 58:10 The Message)

For more information, fill out the form below or email Pastor Nick.

First Name:
Last Name:
Email:
Phone:

I'd like more information on the following Community Service Opportunities:

F.L.I.P (Free Lunch in the Park)
Covenant House (Home for Runaway Teens)
Habitat for Humanity
Serving at a Soup Kitchen

serving during the week

Serving isn't just for Sundays! Each week there are plenty of opportunities to serve in The Journey office. From following up with guests to assembling programs for the Sunday service, investing just one hour makes an eternal difference.

For more information on serving during the week, email Christel.

Invest just one hour in serving this week and make an eternal difference!

Name:
Email:
Phone Number:

Sign me up for:

Super Service Mondays

Super Service Thursdays

Serving During the Day

I am available to serve the following times during the day:

regular server position description

Regular Server—Commit to serving once a month as a part of our setup/teardown team or as an usher, greeter, program distributer, etc.

Will be responsible for:

- Record keeping—who's coming to serve
- Watching to see who did a good job serving
- Personally following up with those who served
- Securing regular serving dates (for the next two months) for those who previously served

Example email:

Hey [First Name],
*   Thank you so much for serving at The Journey on Sunday. Your time of service made a huge impact on everyone who attended!*
*   In addition to serving once a month with your Growth Group, would you be willing to serve during any of the Sundays listed below?*

___ October 25	___ November 29
___ November 1	___ December 6
___ November 8	___ December 13
___ November 15	___ December 20
___ November 22	

Let me know if there's anything that I can do for you.
Thank you for your willingness to serve.

Blessings,
[First Name]

Other Regular Serving Positions Include:

- **Truck Driver**—pick up truck at 6:45 and drive to high school (a person could commit to doing this twice a month)
- **Special Events Team**—arrive one hour before a special event to help set up (examples include: Newcomers' Reception, Growth Group Leader Training, Membership Class)

service leader position description

Service Leader—Membership is required. Each area of serving as listed in the first-serve opportunities can have a service leader. This includes a service leader for ushers, greeters, resources, offering, info table, the setup team before the first service, and the teardown team after the last service.

1. A service leader commits to serving twice a month during one service. He or she arrives one hour before the start of the service and will help lead the serving meeting by giving the specific instructions pertinent to that particular team for that service.
2. During the service, the service leader will monitor the volunteers to ensure they are serving correctly and to encourage them. During this time the service leader will identify anyone who has served well and give this information to The Journey staff person who is leading the serving area for that service.
3. The service leader may be asked by a Journey staff person to assist in the follow-up with those who served on their team the previous Sunday.

sunday coordinator position description

Sunday Coordinator—Membership is required. Tithing is required. A sit-down meeting with a Journey staff person is required. A signing of a Sunday coordinator covenant is required.

1. A Sunday coordinator is someone who has served as a service leader and shown exemplary leadership skills as determined by The Journey staff person leading the volunteer area.
2. If approved, a Sunday coordinator will commit to serving at least two Sundays a month, for one shift each of these Sundays. The two shifts for Sunday coordinators are 7:00–11:30 am and 10:30 am–3:00 pm.

The Sunday coordinator can lead the serving meetings along with The Journey staff person and oversee all of the service leaders and their areas to ensure a quality serving experience for those who serve as well as ensuring the quality experience provided by our volunteers to all Journey attendees for that particular service.

a follow-up process for volunteers

Celebrate New Volunteers

Send out handwritten thank-you notes to volunteers who serve for the first time (thanking them and encouraging them for their service).

On Sundays—encourage and congratulate volunteers after they complete their first serve and tie their service to the principle of the chain (do this in person before they leave).

Two weeks after first serve (or after they serve twice—Kidz/WAT), send an email out to celebrate! Maybe include a survey of their serving experience and include a list of dates that they can sign up to serve on a regular basis.

Celebrate after a Semester of Service

Have a team meeting (lunch/dinner or orientation) to celebrate their service over the semester.

Celebrate key leaders and volunteers with a gift card (members reception).

Randomly send a gift to key volunteers/leaders.

Celebrate Reproducing Volunteers

Bring a friend day—ask volunteers to come serve with them.

"Ask" seasons—where team/service leaders recommend potential volunteers for each ministry. Maybe challenge team leaders and service leaders to build a team for their area.

BIG days—fall festival, ministry fairs, T-shirt days, gift card days—to encourage current volunteers to invite someone to serve.

a simple strategy
for creating a culture
of serving

Create a Culture of Service with Sunday Serving Teams

1. With teaching on Sundays: identify at the preaching calendar meeting if there will be a Sunday teaching series that will focus on serving (in October of each year).

    a. Schedule personal testimonies of serving for each Sunday in the series (six weeks from the beginning of the series).

    b. Schedule a Ministry Fair Sunday during the series (six weeks from the beginning of the series).

    c. Develop the "Next Steps" for each Sunday during the series (two weeks before each specific Sunday).

    d. Write the follow-up emails for each "Next Step" for each Sunday (two weeks before each specific Sunday).

    e. Identify at least one message in each series that focuses on serving (at each teaching team pre-series planning meeting).

    f. Develop the specific serving "Next Step" for the connection card for that Sunday (two weeks before the specific Sunday).

    g. Schedule a personal testimony of serving for the specific Sunday (six weeks from the Sunday).

2. With classes and trainings: reinforce the culture of service and sign people up to serve (finalize two weeks before each class or training).
   a. Membership Class: list out the specific dates of the next eight Sundays along with service times and ask everyone to sign up for two dates.
   b. Newcomers Reception: list out the specific dates of the next four Sundays along with service times and ask everyone to sign up for one date.
   c. Serving Meeting: list out the specific dates of the next four Sundays along with service times and ask everyone to sign up for one date.

3. With communication beyond preaching and classes: clearly communicate the serving opportunities for individuals that exist at The Journey (update each week at ministry meeting).
   a. Each Sunday at the free resource table, have at least one message on the importance and/or value of serving.
   b. Each Sunday at The Journey info table, have the "Serving @ The Journey" brochures clearly displayed.
   c. Develop a "Serving" page similar to the Growth Groups page that has descriptions for each serving position and allows individuals to sign up to serve for a specific position for a specific service.
   d. Write the automatic emails for each serving position that would be sent to someone when they sign up.
   e. Develop a "Serving @ The Journey" button that can be displayed on the home page of the website when we want to highlight serving.

the sunday volunteer experience process

On-Site Experience: When an individual arrives to serve, every effort is made to create an enjoyable experience for the volunteer as well as to communicate the impact that his or her serving is having.

1. Welcome/Orientation: At each serving meeting, there should be an enthusiastic welcome that thanks everyone and explains the salvation chain.
2. Food/Snacks: Where allowed, there should be snacks and drinks for volunteers at each serving meeting.
3. Identifying Volunteers: Where needed, there should be name tags and/or badges and/or T-shirts that clearly label volunteers along with the area that they are serving in.
4. Instructions: At each serving meeting, there should be clear instructions given to everyone who is serving so that they understand their role and how to best fulfill it.
5. Recognition/Encouragement: While serving, each volunteer should be thanked, encouraged, or coached by the service team leader, Sunday coordinator, or Journey staff person to reinforce the value of serving.
6. Post-serving: Each volunteer should be thanked for his or her service that Sunday.

growth group serving reminder email

Subject—REMINDER: Your Growth Group Is Scheduled to Serve THIS Sunday, October 30!

Hey [First Name],

Just a reminder, your Growth Group is scheduled to serve THIS SUNDAY, October 30, during the 6:30 pm service at our Village Location—PS 41 (116 W 11th St.—between 6th & 7th Avenues).

Your Growth Group will be serving together, so it will be a great way to get to know the other members in your group.

Hope to see you Sunday!

—Rebecca

P.S. You will still get to hear this Sunday's message since you will only be serving during the first twenty minutes of the service. We are continuing our "God on Film" series. See you there!

sunday serving meeting outline (pep talk)

AN OUTLINE FOR A VOLUNTEER MEETING

Serving Meeting Outline

  I. Hello/Introductions
  II. Memory verse
  III. What the message is about this week
  IV. How the message pertains to serving
  V. Why serving is important at The Journey
    a. Read first-time guest comments
      i. Serving helps you feel better about yourself
        1. VERSE: What good is it if a man gains the whole world, yet forfeits his soul?
        2. It is what God commands us to do
        a. Inspiring story
  VI. Please fill out the information provided on the back of the card
  VII. Love to have you as a regular server
    a. Regular servers serve just once a month, which equals an hour per month
    b. You can choose what team you will be on, ushers, greeters, resources
  VII. Prayer
  IX. Hand out assignments

ideas to inspire volunteers during the serving meeting (pep talk)

1. Share testimonies on how your Growth Group is doing.
   a. For example, I had one volunteer share how a GG member got her a job!
2. Take an inspiring quote and hand it out to the group.
3. Share inspiring stories with your group.
   a. I like to use stories I've found on blogs, stories on how volunteering has changed people's lives—specifically at The Journey, etc.
4. Go around the circle and share one thing you're grateful for.
5. Emphasize how Jesus was the greatest servant of all and serving helps us become more like him.
6. Get a volunteer to share how serving impacted their first experience at The Journey.
7. Emphasize how much of an impact we make by serving in the front of house area.
   a. You are one of the first faces people will see as they come into The Journey.

serving thank-you email

Subject: Thank You!

Hey [First Name],

Thank you for serving yesterday! It was fun serving with you and I know that you had an impact on all the people who came to the service.

I would love to have you come volunteer with us again on Sunday. Would you be interested in serving again?

Serving is a great way to develop friendships and grow spiritually. I also like to think we have some fun too! ☺

Like I was saying yesterday, volunteering once a month is only an hour commitment for the entire month . . .

Can you just email me three dates in June, July, and August when you are available to serve again?

I'm looking forward to serving with you more!

—Rebecca

email to those who have confirmed a place of service

Subject: Serving with the Welcome Team

Hi [First Name],

My name is Rebecca, and I am the director of volunteers at The Journey! I saw that you checked on your connection card that you're interested in serving, so I wanted to follow up.

I also wanted to share this verse with you: "God has given each of you a gift from his great variety of spiritual gifts. Use them well to serve one another" (1 Pet. 4:10).

I'm excited that you have decided to use your spiritual gifts to serve with us. Serving is really easy—all you have to do is arrive one hour before the service you usually attend. From there, we will have a serving meeting and I will show you exactly what to do. We have several positions, such as greeting, passing out programs, and ushering, so if you have a preference, just let me know.

Would you be able to join me this Sunday, October 30? There are a lot of exciting things happening this Sunday, so it would be a perfect day for you to come and volunteer with us!

Just send me an email confirming you will be there, along with the service you will be attending. If you can't make it

Sunday, no worries, just let me know another date you are available to serve.

Thanks!

—Rebecca

email to those who checked "serving" on their connection card

Subject: Will You Join Me Sunday?

Hey [First Name],

My name is Rebecca and I am the director of volunteers at The Journey! I saw that you filled out on your second-time guest survey that you were interested in serving, and I wanted to follow up!

I wanted to see if you could join me this Sunday (June 26). There are a lot of exciting things happening this Sunday, so it would be a perfect day for you to come and volunteer with us!

It's really easy—just show up an hour before the service you normally attend and meet me in our volunteer area in the lobby.

It's a great way to meet other people in the church, and I like to think it's a lot of fun. ☺

We will have a volunteer meeting and then I'll get you started serving, plus I'll have coffee and donuts there for all the volunteers.

Once you are finished serving, you can go right on into the auditorium and enjoy the service.

Will you join me on Sunday? Just send me an email confirming you will be there, along with the service you will be attending. I would love to have you serve with us!

Excited to serve with you,

Rebecca

fully engaged in my church

(A SAMPLE SERMON OUTLINE ON SERVING)

NELSON SEARCY, LEAD PASTOR

The eyes of the LORD search the whole earth in order to strengthen those whose hearts are fully committed to him.

—2 Chronicles 16:9

Five Actions of a Fully Engaged Life

1. I <u>Take Responsibility</u> Daily for My Spiritual Growth

   Come close to God, and God will come close to you. Wash your hands, you sinners; purify your hearts, for your loyalty is divided between God and the world. (James 4:8)

2. I <u>Practice Contentment</u> in All Areas of My Life

   I know what it is to be in need, and I know what it is to have plenty. I have learned the secret of being content in any and every situation, whether well fed or hungry, whether living in plenty or in want. (Phil. 4:12 NIV)

3. I <u>Serve One Hour a Week</u> in My Church (Minimum)

   Anyone who wants to be my disciple must follow me, because my servants must be where I am. And the Father will honor anyone who serves me. (John 12:26)

The greatest among you must be a servant. (Matt. 23:11)

4. I Invite Three Friends a Month to Church with Me

Devote yourselves to prayer, being watchful and thankful. And pray for us, too, that God may open a door for our message, so that we may proclaim the mystery of Christ, for which I am in chains. Pray that I may proclaim it clearly, as I should. Be wise in the way you act toward outsiders; make the most of every opportunity. Let your conversation be always full of grace, seasoned with salt, so that you may know how to answer everyone. (Col. 4:2–6 NIV)

5. I Bring the Full Tithe to God Each Week

"Bring the whole tithe into the storehouse, that there may be food in my house. Test me in this," says the LORD Almighty, "and see if I will not throw open the floodgates of heaven and pour out so much blessing that you will not have room enough to store it." (Mal. 3:10 NIV)

Wherever your treasure is, there the desires of your heart will also be. (Matt. 6:21)

By their fruit you will recognize them. Do people pick grapes from thornbushes, or figs from thistles? Likewise every good tree bears good fruit, but a bad tree bears bad fruit. (Matt. 7:16–17 NIV)

My Next Step Today Is To:

Memorize 2 Chronicles 16:9.

Commit now to live out all five Actions of Engagement.

Sign up to serve in my church: __ Sunday __ Monday __ Thursday.

Accept the four-month Tithe Challenge (send me the free resource).

Below the Next Step Box:

Sign me up for Growth Group # _____

Nelson Searcy is the founding lead pastor of The Journey Church of the City with locations in New York City, Queens, Brooklyn, and Boca Raton, FL. He is also the founder of www.ChurchLeaderInsights.com. He and his church appear routinely on lists such as the 50 Most Influential Churches and the 25 Most Innovative Leaders. Searcy lives in New York City.

For Your Church Members:
MOTIVATION *to* SERVE

The Greatness Principle, a perfect companion to *Connect*, is designed specifically with the individual believer in mind. Priced right for small groups and church-wide campaigns, this little book packs a wealth of practical insight and inspired ideas that will energize church members and have them clamoring to volunteer their talents for the sake of the kingdom.

For leaders, the perfect companion to
The Greatness Principle

Worship as One—
UNITE MEMBERS *and* LEADERS

For Worship Leaders

Engage, the church leaders' companion to *Revolve*, is a step-by-step, stress-free guide to planning worship services that allow for and foster true life change. Comprehensive in scope, *Engage* provides teaching pastors, worship leaders, and volunteers the tools they need to work together to develop and implement a worship planning system that improves communication, enhances creativity, and honors Jesus every week.

For Church Members

With *Revolve*, church members will see that when they approach worship with a "what can I get out of this" attitude, they're bound to be disappointed. However, worshiping God as a way of life not only honors God but also satisfies our souls. Built-in action steps at the end of each short chapter will give readers specific ideas about how to refocus their attention on God and live each day in an attitude of worship.

The Ultimate How-to Book for
REACHING MORE
PEOPLE *for* JESUS CHRIST

"*Ignite* is creative, practical, and interesting. Nelson Searcy, founder and senior pastor of The Journey Church in New York City, provides helpful ideas on growing a church through using Big Days, or what some might call Big Events. Readers will find insights to put into immediate practice in their churches, and they'll enjoy reading the book. Searcy is one of the two or three top young practitioners and writers on evangelism and church growth for the twenty-first century."—*Outreach*

BakerBooks

Available wherever books are sold.

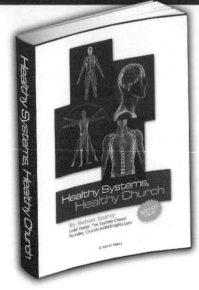